DECOLONIZE SELF-CARE

Forthcoming in the *Decolonize That!* series

Decolonize Multiculturalism by Anthony C. Alessandrini
Decolonize Drag by Kareem Khubchandani

DECOLONIZE
SELF-CARE

ALYSON K. SPURGAS
ZOË C. MELEO-ERWIN

OR Books
New York · London

The *Decolonize That!* series is produced by OR Books in collaboration with *Warscapes* magazine.

© 2023 Alyson K. Spurgas and Zoë C. Meleo-Erwin

Published by OR Books, New York and London
Visit our website at www.orbooks.com

All rights information: rights@orbooks.com

First printing 2023

Cataloging-in-Publication data is available from the Library of Congress. A catalog record for this book is available from the British Library.

Typeset by Lapiz Digital Services.

paperback ISBN 978-1-68219-335-8 • ebook ISBN 978-1-68219-336-5

CONTENTS

EDITOR'S PREFACE

We've all gone down that virtual rabbit hole: scrolling and scrolling, eyes and thumb glued to the phone. And because your social media knows you so well, you're sure to find it: that perfectly articulated and instantly empowering meme-quote.

It will most likely be some version of Snoop Dogg's heavily lip-synced viral song, "I Wanna Thank Me," where he not only thanks himself for believing in himself but also reminds himself of his own upright and charitable personality. Unfortunately, your meme-quote will lack Snoop's humor as well as his allusion to his years of hard work, but it will still be the thing you need right there, right now.

You'll find this meme-quote around the time you're feeling unappreciated at work, despairing from not losing weight on your new diet, and seeing a spike in casual sexism all around you ('cos you're probably a cis woman). The meme-quote will tell you that you matter, that you deserve happiness, that you are manifesting a resilient, purposeful, and empowered you. You are the boss of you. Urgently, it will tell you that self-care is the thing you need right now. At least momentarily, you will be convinced by these truths. Even if you're a cynic or an anti-capitalist rebel, you'll probably find the peppy meme harmless enough that you might follow a bunch of self-care accounts, subscribe to a new exercise program or a meditation app. Maybe you will even splurge on one of those constantly advertised feminist bras: the ones that support your boobs *and* the revolution.

In *Decolonize Self-Care,* Alyson K. Spurgas and Zoë Meleo-Erwin offer an accurate diagnosis of all of the above: "People today are overworked, exhausted, worn down, and many (hello!) are full of rage—as we should be! Care is something so many of us desperately need." And nothing like a dangerous, global pandemic to remind us just how much we need this. As I write this on a random Tuesday morning, the hashtag "selfcare" has been used in 57.8 million posts on Instagram. It would be a cop-out to simply say that social media turns us into fools, and it behooves us to view this fury of posts as a cry for help from people who hope to improve their lives. Yet these social media posts offering quick fixes are not the solution, and these empty signifiers show us that something is irreparably broken in existing systems for care and wellness.

In their thoughtful and considerate book, Alyson and Zoë are not only cognizant of our collective despair, but are trying to figure out why none of this is working. Why is there so much self-care all around us, but so little good health, relief, or peace? *Decolonize Self-Care* exposes this extractive, capitalist racket by showing, for starters, that "contemporary self-care industries are deeply out of touch with the types of care that many people actually require and are clamoring for." Self-care is an integral ingredient in everything from brands by mega-influencers Gwyneth Paltrow and Kim Kardashian; to the promotion of Girl Bosses, FemTech divas, and women entrepreneurs; to the proliferation of "painmoons" and "extreme travel"; to several diets using dog-whistle terms like "clean," "ancient," or "paleolithic"; to mindfulness programs that optimize women's "inherent" productivity, mindful eating, mindful breathing, and mindful sexuality. Self-care is also a component of that most elusive of products on the market today: the female orgasm.

Self-care has been on a pretty twisted journey since Audre Lorde first crafted the idea almost thirty-five years ago. "Caring for myself is not self-indulgence, it is self-preservation, and that is an act of political warfare," declared this Black, lesbian, socialist feminist at a time when she was coping with breast cancer. As the authors of this book make clear, what we seem to have really stuck with today is the "self" part. The "political warfare" bit, the part that insists on self-care as community care, and what they call the "revolutionary movements that connected care, health, and wellness to broader efforts for change," have been largely lost in the crude neoliberal hustle to make a quick buck (or maybe a quick million) primarily from capitalizing on people's poor physical and mental health. There is abundant irony here too: the same hustle that demands you work overtime and causes you extraordinary stress can be alleviated by the self-care hustle.

Self-care's inherent neoliberalism and its profit-facing, get-rich-from-people's-despair tendency may not need much unpacking, but its connections to colonization and decolonization are often not immediately visible. Yet the math is simple: the Lorde version of self-care was decolonial at its core but today, in becoming an industry preying upon women and queer populations, it has literally sold its soul. Decolonizing, dismantling, and resisting self-care is more urgent than it appears.

Colonial ideology relies heavily on a system of binaries: civilized/uncivilized, master/slave, masculine/feminine, and normative/queer. Marxist feminist scholar Maria Mies explains it best: "The predatory patriarchal division of labor is based, from the outset, on a structural separation and subordination of human beings: men are separated from women, whom they have subordinated, their 'own' people are separated from the 'foreigners' or 'heathens.'" This system forms the "hidden foundation" of colonial society. These binaries remain entrenched in our collective consciousness to this day and manifest themselves whether at home, at work, or unfortunately, in your own sense of self. The three interconnected C's (colonialism, capitalism, christianity) that have wrecked two-thirds of the planet created this foundation by violently controlling and subordinating their "own" and "other" women and actively erasing other genders.

European men kept European women subjugated through a rigorous network of economic, religious, civil, and psychological institutions. Let me remind you of "Lie back and think of England." A phrase that allegedly originated in Victorian times speaks volumes about making heterosexual intercourse tolerable for women by reminding women of their duty to produce sons for a rapidly expanding Empire. These same white/Western women produced the next rung of domination by tyrannizing native, enslaved, or colonized women in colonial outposts and in settler colonies. In these gendered spaces, control was often exercised through direct violence, but not always. Civilizing "other" women through the enforcement of hygiene, wellness, diet, dressing, medicine, and behavior was an important part of European women's pious and feminine colonial agenda.

Decolonize Self-Care takes us on a journey that is as incredibly illuminating as it is shocking. It is shocking to find out that in the first quarter of the twenty-first century, we are still captive to a heteronormative patriarchy that controls women's bodies to such a vast degree. It is less shocking but still despairing to see the extent to which a white, saviorist, and neoliberal feminism continues to exploit racialized and gendered populations. We will learn that gender and sexuality cannot be afterthoughts in the decolonizing mission; nor can the food we eat, or the types of self-healing we may find ourselves gravitating towards.

A singular, brilliant aspect of *Decolonize Self-Care* is that it doesn't just stop at complaint and critique, but offers a path to radicalizing your understanding and practice of care. "More care, less self," they say, and by the time we get to the end of the book, we'll find out exactly how that is possible.

Bhakti Shringarpure
February 2022

INTRODUCTION

Care for Yourself Like the "Likes" Depend on It

It was late February 2020, and the global COVID-19 pandemic was slowly starting to become a *pretty big deal* in the United States. We remember going about our lives in New York City as we had always done, but also noticing subtle shifts—there seemed to be just slightly more anxiety in the air than usual. The novel coronavirus was becoming an increasingly frequent topic of conversation in the news and in our personal and professional circles; certain cleaning and paper products were becoming more difficult to find, and yet city, state, and federal officials were downplaying conditions. In fact, on March 3—two days after the first confirmed case of COVID-19 in New York state—New York City mayor Bill de Blasio encouraged New Yorkers to go on with life as normal. That was cool by us. At the time, we probably would have seen any restrictions on regular life as an annoyance—New Yorkers' fast-paced, busy lifestyles are almost a cliché, after all . . .

Four days later, New York governor Andrew Cuomo would declare a state of emergency.

Around this same time, on February 26 to be exact, the actress and influencer Gwyneth Paltrow, who owns and runs the infamous Goop lifestyle wellness company, posted a selfie on Instagram. In the image, she was adorned with a sleek Airinium brand face mask (starting at $75) and a comfy-looking eye cover. The post read: "En Route to Paris. Paranoid? Prudent? Panicked? Placid? Pandemic? Propaganda? Paltrow's just going to go ahead and sleep with this thing on the plane. I've already been in this movie [here she is referencing the 2011 viral disaster apocalyptic film "Contagion"]. Stay safe. Don't shake hands. Wash hands frequently."

Immediately after the post, news sites began to write snarky think pieces in response: the *Los Angeles Times* caught wind of the Instagram post the same day, and *The New York Times* published a short article in its Style section entitled "The Rich Are Preparing for Coronavirus Differently" soon after on March 5. But perhaps most importantly for our discussion of *self-care as lifestyle* is that the mask Paltrow was wearing quickly sold out, despite the fact that, at the time, public health officials were encouraging citizens not to wear masks so that they could be saved for health care workers. And that mask remained sold out for months on end.

Fast-forward eight months to the end of October 2020. Over 8.7 million Americans had been infected with COVID-19 and over 225,000 had died. Once again, a high-profile influencer made the news with a gauche comment about "self-care" on Instagram. This time the culprit was Kim Kardashian, who shared some lovely glamour shots from a private island to which she flew members of her inner circle (after "health screens" and quarantining, of course) to celebrate her fortieth birthday and "pretend things were normal just for a brief moment in time." Social media responses to Kardashian's tweets and posts were swift and ranged from the very sarcastic ("What, you weren't able to fly to a private island with the $1200 stimulus check you got 6 months ago?!") to the more defensive ("Worry about controlling your own destiny rather than judging others for the privileges they worked for. Who wouldn't party on a private island if they could?"). For the record, we also found ourselves rolling our eyes at these grotesque social media displays while simultaneously wishing we were on the posh vacay with Kim or the private jet with Gwyneth.

Notably, our illustrious influencer Kim Kardashian also made a point to check herself by stating "I am humbly reminded how privileged my life is." In fact, the words "humbled" and "blessed" were used multiple times throughout the post, and she went to great lengths to acknowledge that her experience was "so far out of reach for most people" during the hellscape of 2020. She added, "Before COVID I don't think any of us truly appreciated what a simple luxury it was to be able to travel and be together with family and friends in a safe environment." We wonder if Kardashian realizes that not only is her lavish birthday celebration out of reach for many people during the restrictions of a global pandemic, but that many people cannot regularly see their friends and family or travel even during non-pandemic times. Despite her repeated attempts at virtue-signaling (more on that in a moment), she was thoroughly lambasted and lampooned on social media. One tweet raised how ridiculous it was to even use the words "normal" and "private island" in the same sentence. Many expressed distress at how woefully out-of-touch Kardashian appeared to be. Memes abounded.

Even the #humble and "stay safe" parts of Kardashian's and Paltrow's posts ring hollow as performances of wokeness and care in the face of obvious immense privilege. How utterly annoying are these two, posting about jaunting off to Paris and private islands to escape from it all while most of us are suffering through the pandemic in quite a different manner? But as much as we enjoy some good ol' fashioned hate-scrolling and snarky think pieces roasting elites, we also believe that influencers and celebrities like Kim Kardashian and Gwyneth Paltrow are really just symptoms of larger problems related to the commodification of self-care, woke wellness, and hashtag profiteering more broadly that too many of us are complicit in. In a sense, then, these particular white women celebrities seem to have become scapegoats.

Kardashian's and Paltrow's gaudy versions of self-care and wellness are lifestyles aspirational to many yet accessible to few. But at the same time, self-care appears to be everywhere, at a price point even *you* can afford! Herein lies one paradox of contemporary self-care: Though the most elite versions of self-care are, of course, *the best*, if you can't afford those versions, you can approximate their benefits (and, frankly, you should try!) by taking advantage of the vast marketplace that has been designed for exactly this purpose. That is, you may not have the funds for a private island birthday adventure with a gorgeous entourage to enjoy a night swim with, but you can almost certainly afford some affirmation cards, "hidden message mantra" bracelet cuffs (no, seriously), or essential oils ordered from Amazon. Even better: just get the Calm app for free. Haute self-care for the elites and bargain-basement self-care for the commoners—what a time to be alive!

Contemporary self-care tends to center a certain kind of ostentatious *wokeness*, or, according to Urban Dictionary, "the act of being very pretentious about how much you care about a social issue." But this often seems to amount to little more than *virtue signaling* ("taking a conspicuous but essentially useless action ostensibly to support a good cause but actually to show off how much more moral you are than everybody else," also according to Urban Dictionary). So, the second paradox of contemporary self-care that we want to highlight in this book is this: self-care regimens today are more likely than ever to emphasize "social justice," "community care," and even the importance of "the political." Yet, as they do so, many of these regimes are still largely constrained by an unchecked individualism, and actually end up perpetuating social and economic inequality.

People today are overworked, exhausted, worn down, and many (hello!) are full of rage—as we should be! Care is something so many of us desperately need. But, at the same time, contemporary self-care industries are deeply out of touch with the types of care that many people actually require and are clamoring for. Today's self-care messages range from: "Do self-care because you will become a more efficient entrepreneur" to "Do self-care because it's the right thing to do for your community and the world" to the more basic mantra (which connects the first two) "Do self-care because you'll *feel* better—and be your authentic/empowered/ultra-Zen self(!)—if you do."

But in each of these messages, the self-carer is always the one who singularly benefits: you might grow your own personal brand and achieve financial success, feeling calm and centered while doing so, in the first example, or you may acquire other mental health benefits, including an overall feeling of goodwill or connection, higher self-esteem, and lower anxiety because you did something positive for the world, in the last example. This is to say, even while using the language of "community" and "social justice" (and, as we'll discuss, often "diversity" and "inclusion"), today's versions of self-care offer some benefits but don't go nearly far enough to alter the social conditions that make us feel like shit in the first place. In this sense, they are a Band-Aid, at best—and at worst, they further entrench existing and unequal structures of power by emphasizing individualist solutions to what are ultimately systemic problems.

To be clear: When we say "existing structures of power" and "systemic problems," we mean intersecting forms of inequality, including white supremacy, nationalism, sexism, homophobia, transphobia, and ableism, all of which are historically and contemporarily intertwined, and all of which originate with and/or are exacerbated by capitalism. These forms of oppression are further connected to colonialism and the processes by which white Europeans have subjugated (and continue to subjugate) everyone else.

Following decolonial theorists Eve Tuck and K. Wayne Yang, we might further differentiate between *external* colonialism and *internal* colonialism—the former being predicated on the extraction of indigenous resources, including human beings, to build wealth and power for colonizing nations, while the latter involves modes of control and subjugation of people, land, and animals *within* an imperial nation. Importantly for us, given our concern with self-care commodification and how it travels, the United States, as a settler colonial nation, is an example of both. While contemporary coloniality may differ in design and execution than historical forms, the key here is that overall systems of domination and exploitation are ongoing, with negative material, cultural, psychological, and health effects, particularly for Black and Indigenous people of color (BIPOC).

Importantly, coloniality is not sustained through physical force alone but also through ideas and practices, particularly those related to economic and government policy. Our understandings of reality are deeply shaped by these intersecting forces. That is, these forces shape our ideas of what is and isn't a problem (for instance a social, economic, or health problem), what causes said problem, who is responsible for addressing it, and what should be done. In highly unequal social and economic systems, regardless of intent, the *impact* of ideas and practices—including those related to self-care—can reproduce the status quo, in general, and coloniality (relations of power, domination, and exploitation rooted in Eurocentrism and white supremacy), in specific.

In the United States, the work of decolonization, or the sustained undoing of these matrices of power, domination, and exploitation, has been ongoing since European conquerors first set foot upon Turtle Island (the term commonly used by many Indigenous people, particularly in northeastern areas, to refer to the North American continent)—a struggle born of necessity. At a basic level, decolonization involves: an intellectual and emotional grappling with the ecological destruction and human suffering first wrought by coloniality in the name of profit and power; an understanding of the fact that in the United States, Indigenous peoples as well as those of African descent have been (and still are) the target of and suffer most from these genocidal and exploitative processes even though these processes ultimately harm everyone to different degrees; a redefinition and redistribution of wealth and land as a means by which to begin addressing these atrocities; and a radical rethinking and reconfiguring of both social relations and societal institutions in order to promote collective well-being. Finally, it requires a dismantling of whiteness, which was never a true indicator of ancestry, but rather a form of securing and disseminating power and property.

Just as coloniality is ongoing, decolonization is not an endpoint, but a process—one that seeks to shed light upon existing systems of power and open up the possibilities of different ways of being in the world. And decolonizing is quite literally vital, as existing systems of power, though we are all positioned differently within them, are toxic for all of us and the planet at large.

In service of such decolonizing, we hope to illustrate how and why self-care markets are not the best way forward, as they perpetuate toxic relations borne out of white supremacy, elitism, and capitalism—just with a "softer" and "gentler" veneer, and increasingly in the terms of (wealthy, white) "girl power." Even as we express serious qualms with this, we also want to highlight that the conversation around self-care has shifted immensely in the last few years, and particularly during the COVID-19 pandemic and subsequent racial justice movements of the year 2020. Something certainly does feel new about Kim Kardashian acknowledging her privilege on Instagram, especially at a time when key self-care and wellness companies are now regularly talking about diversity, equity, inclusion, and health disparities.

We are not here to downplay the importance of these evolving conversations and the concomitant steps some of these influencers, celebrities, companies, etc. are now attempting toward social change. We do want to be realistic, though, about what has actually changed, what has not, and, most importantly, about the ways in which care is being pushed in more radical directions by social movements from the ground up. Thus, we note the contradictions that surround self-care, and we honor the powerful organizing that has ensured that groups who need it most have access to the care they need. Throughout this book, we also describe different *phases* of self-care—but we note that they are overlapping and not completely distinct. In fact, these different iterations of or historical moments within self-care discourse follow from each other in ways that are, as we will explain, not that surprising when you think about it.

On these final points, our grasp of the radical potential of care, as well as the larger contexts that shape and surround more mainstream, contemporary self-care movements are made possible by and founded upon the painstaking work of organizers, activists, scholars, and artists, particularly BIPOC, disabled, queer, and trans individuals who grapple with these issues and whom we mention throughout this book. We are indebted to their work, and we are grateful for the gifts that their labor—borne out of necessity and survival—has given the world.

A Brief Note on Method: "We'll have an oat milk turmeric latte, two sides of a free-range autoimmune condition, some extra anxiety, and a full order of grass-fed revolution, to go!"

This project began the way that many feminist and social justice collaborations do—over shared meals and cups of coffee. During the last few years, we—friends from graduate school, both still living in New York City—got together on a number of occasions to catch up. Our conversations wove seamlessly between multiple topics: the stress and pressures of academia (both as faced by ourselves, as pre-tenure academics, and those faced by our students), our intimate relationships, grad school gossip (let's be real), larger issues related to inter/national politics and social inequality, and—increasingly—concerns about our own health. On this latter point, we discovered that we both suffered from similar maladies, some of them vague in nature. We felt like we were barely keeping up and we were worried that our efforts to do so were coming at a severe cost to our physical and mental health.

We discussed visiting biomedical providers (those trained in the Western, "allopathic" system of medicine) of various backgrounds who had offered few effective long-term solutions (or at least few solutions that didn't, in turn, come with their own set of, shall we say, "challenges" . . .). Online pop-psych and pop-feminist articles advised such remedies as mindfulness, treating ourselves to spa days and other small pleasures, saying "no" to others and their needs (put yourself first!), scheduling alone time, spending time in nature, practicing gratitude, getting more/better sleep, improving our diet, taking better care of our gut health, "manifesting," and more.

We were doubtful that these were the answers, but we did find ourselves exploring natural remedies and popular diets such as keto and paleo with the hope they would offer some relief. After all, the gut microbiome was clearly having a cultural moment. Could it be the answer to the digestive health and autoimmune conditions that seemed to be everywhere these days—and that we were acutely experiencing, ourselves? Or was it like the human genome at the end of the twentieth century or the brain in the early twenty-first century—emerging areas of study that undoubtedly held some answers, but which were, as explanatory models, overhyped and capitalized upon (puzzles prevent dementia!) in ways that the science did not bear out in the end? The promises of the self-care industry were ones that we felt attracted to and wary of all at once.

Beyond concerns about the evidence base for products and practices that promised increased health and wellness, we were skeptical of the politics and money surrounding self-care. The market and the marketers seemed largely to be white, upper/middle-class, cisgender or cis women (individuals assigned "female" at birth who identify as women). And we noticed that this demographic shift was being hailed as "empowering" and "feminist" in an entrepreneurial "boss-babe," "lady-boss," "earn-your-dream" sort of way. Self-care seemed to be not only a path to healing and resilience, but also a way to climb the ladder of success. We wondered: What did it mean that self-care products and services were being sold in ways that hyped (white) femininity and girl power? When self-care is literally sold, who actually benefits? Who (and where) might this self-care industry harm? What other more communal, collectivist, and radical forms of care are negated—or co-opted—when wellness becomes a brand? And so, this project began.

In addition to our own (gendered) physical and mental health conditions, chronic illnesses, and disabilities, the fact that we have both spent much time in anarcho-communist, anti-racist, and queer feminist collectives, punk communities, and other leftist countercultural spaces also informs our questions and approach toward care throughout this book (as does our training as critical medical sociologists). Further, that we are both relatively privileged white people living in the settler colonial territory known as North America, and New York City (unceded Munsee Lenape and Canarsie land) in particular, certainly shapes our perspectives and the examples we draw upon.

Ok, But What Is "Self-Care" Anyway? And Where Did It Come From?

Over the last few decades, terms such as "wellness" and "self-care" have become more common in households across wealthy countries such as the United States. The two terms are related, though different. "Wellness" is usually understood to be an optimal state of mind, body, spirit and holistic health. As rhetoric of health and medicine scholar Colleen Derkatch elaborates, popular notions of "wellness" seem to rely on two competing ideas—*restoration* (regaining something primal and more-over authentic that has been allegedly lost to the perils of modern life) and *optimization* (enhancing one's potential to be *better than well*). We understand "self-care"—as it is most often portrayed on social media and elsewhere—as the strategies by which one actively works toward both restoration and optimization.

Self-care has its origins in the late-twentieth-century shifting relationship between patients and the field of medicine, wherein individuals were increasingly encouraged by policy makers, medical providers, and employers to assume greater personal responsibility for their own positive health outcomes through the assessment of individual risk, lifestyle changes, and active engagement with the health care system.

These days, the whole idea of self-care is most commonly associated with individualized and indulgent activities that people (particularly women) do—or are expected to do—"because we deserve it." This includes things like taking a bath, getting a massage, meditating, doing yoga, going on a vacation, or even sleeping late. Self-care has also become synonymous with its expression on social media. Such posts and tweets might include a photo of the self-carer doing some type of pampering activity—maybe she bought a special beverage at Starbucks, for example—along with the hashtag

"#SelfCareSunday" (or is it "#SelfCareSaturday"? We can't keep up anymore . . .). Before we do a deep dive into the contemporary market-friendly self-help, health, and wellness landscape, though, there's another history of self-care that's important to think about—an origin story wherein the concept seems to mean something quite different.

Let's begin with the Black queer poet and social-ist feminist Audre Lorde, oft cited (and meme-ified) in relation to self-care. In 1988, four years before her death, Lorde famously stated, "Caring for myself is not self-indulgence, it is self-preservation, and that is an act of political warfare." Really take in that last part of her statement—"an act of *political warfare*." With this, she is suggesting that self-care is an inherently political act, and that caring for oneself has broader social ramifica-tions. Lorde was contending not only with intersecting oppressions due to white supremacy, classism, sexism, and homophobia, but also with breast cancer, and she viewed her own personal survival and the survival of her communities as intertwined. Effectively, she was argu-ing that we must engage in acts of self-care not only to heal ourselves, but so that we can continue to fight for social justice. Even before Lorde's work clarified the old feminist mantra "the personal is political," there were other revolutionary movements that connected care, health, and wellness to broader efforts for change. Briefly exploring this history serves as a reminder—including of the pitfalls and problems that can crop up within even the most well-intentioned care and justice movements.[1]

In the 1960s, the Black Panther Party (BPP), which was popularly associated with "violence" due to its radical anti-government, anti-capitalist, anti-white supremacist, self-defense and community-defense stance, was a serious advocate of caring for the health of community members, including children. Examples of this include the Panthers' initiation of community-based before-school breakfast programs and sickle cell anemia screening efforts to address the unmet needs of Black people living in the US. Although their original 1966 *Ten-Point Program* did not explicitly highlight health as a formal demand of the United States government, in the early 1970s, the Panthers instituted community health centers around the country and improving health became integral to the Party platform. Eventually a

---

1   See Hobart & Kneese (2020), Hanna (2020), and Seiler (2020) for more on the complexities of care in light of gender, race, and sexuality differences (and associated power imbalances) among members of social justice movements. For instance, Black women members of the BPP have critiqued the sexism and misogyny that some saw as emanating unchecked from men in the group. This is only one example of the contradictions that abound within radical organizations.

demand for free health care for all oppressed peoples was added to the official program. For the BPP, access to free health care, including preventative care, was necessary to address and moreover survive the illnesses, ailments, and traumas that were endemic to life under the oppression of white supremacy and capitalist economic inequality in the settler colonial United States of America.

In this way, social conditions, institutionalized medicine, community health, self-determination/-defense, and community- and self-care were thoroughly intertwined. It is worth noting that the Panthers' linking of structural conditions such as (un)employment, governance, surveillance, neighborhood conditions, access to public and medical services, and raced/classed social relations to quality of health prefigured what would come to be known in the fields of public health and sociology as "social determinants of health" and "health disparities"; when social and health scientists use these terms, they mean the non-biological/non-behavioral factors that determine community health outcomes and health inequities between groups of people.[2]

2 An even earlier connection between these phenomena comes from the turn of the century scholar-activist W. E. B. Du Bois (1899) who published an extensive case study, *The Philadelphia Negro,* on the connections between larger societal conditions, health status, and life chances of African Americans in 1899.

Like the BPP, The Young Lords—a Latinx racial and economic justice organization formed in New York City in the 1960s—also focused on the relationship between self, community, health, and care as a fundamental part of social change. As part of their activist work, they organized such services as door-to-door lead-poisoning and tuberculosis tests, clothing programs, health care, daycare services, community dinners, and free breakfast programs for neighborhood young people. When youth came in for breakfast, they were offered radical educational reading materials that were written in their native languages, and about their native cultures.[3]

Reproductive health and justice-centered feminist movements have also consistently focused on self-care as part of community care and survival. In the 1960s, underground abortion networks like the Abortion Counseling Service of Women's Liberation proliferated covertly around the United States. Colloquially known as the Jane Collective, one group operated out of Chicago in the late 1960s and early 1970s, prior to the landmark US Supreme Court case—*Roe v. Wade*—that made abortion temporarily legal from 1973 to 2022. In the face of a punishing conservative political climate

3   For more on The Young Lords, see http://palante.org/AboutYoung-Lords.htm.

that relegated individuals to deal with their pregnancies whether they wanted them or not, members of underground abortion networks like Jane taught themselves the basics of abortion care (using technologies like homemade dilation and curettage [D & C] tools, cannulas, and other self-/friend-administrable methods). They also put the word out about their do-it-yourself (DIY) services so that others could avail themselves of these services.[4]

Due to the fact that this type of reproductive care has been systematically neglected, made inaccessible, and often criminalized, it makes sense that folks with uteruses/ovaries across racial and class backgrounds were some of the first to take on this work (people with these gestational organs and those who identify as women have also disproportionately been midwives, doulas, and healers of various sorts). As with the Panthers and the Young Lords, abortion rights activists like the members of Jane had to figure out ways to take care of themselves

---

4   The use of these tactics—in addition to abortifacient oral medications and herbs—has been ongoing, as many individuals with uteruses around the country could not easily access clinical surgical abortions even after *Roe*'s passage in 1973. Now, in the wake of the SCOTUS *Dobbs v. Jackson Women's Health Organization* decision in 2022, these methods will undoubtedly proliferate even further and take new forms.

and each other because their health needs were violently ignored by the health care system writ large, as well as by federal and state governments. In defending their own and each other's health and lives in this way, these activists challenged the authority of medical professionals whose expertise had long been considered sacrosanct.

In spite of the revolutionary anti-racist, feminist, and working-class underpinnings of these early and often overlapping movements in the US (other mid-late twentieth century social justice movements that focused on community care include the queer liberation and HIV/AIDS movements, the disability rights movement, and the trans rights and radical disability justice movements), the agendas of white, middle-class, cis women too often shaped the strategies and goals of reproductive rights and sexual health activism, and thus these women disproportionately benefited from these forms of care. Historian of science and gender studies scholar Michelle Murphy calls this imbalance of care in the name of empowerment *protocol feminism*—a feminism "invested in the politics of technique," including in self-help optimization strategies and DIY enhancements of the (white, cis female) body. Protocol feminism is contradictory: it advocates for "revolution," "radical politics," and "taking the power back," while simultaneously being a product of and firmly entrenched within the status-quo inequalities of capitalism, white supremacy, and dominant biomedical technologies.

On first glance, this type of feminism might appear to have simply co-opted the radical origins of self-care, instead making it all about, for example, white cis women examining their vaginas with mirrors (a la the feminist self-help and women's health movements that became so popular in the US in the 1970s—the living room, or more often the group of women and their specific self-help protocol, *became* the clinic). However, the story is a bit more complicated than overt co-optation—and we are certainly not arguing that "knowing your body" isn't important! Of course it is, and everyone should have access to this knowledge, rather than it being under the control of (disproportionately white male) medical experts. In fact, that's the point—it makes sense that lots of women, across race and class backgrounds, wanted to cultivate this self-knowledge, help themselves and each other, and craft a more revolutionary protocol for self-care.

But: it is also imperative to remember that not all reproductive and sexual health struggles for care are or have ever been the same; by contrast, knowing "our bodies/ourselves,"[5] or even securing access to safe and legal abortion, were often *not* the biggest reproductive sovereignty and autonomy concerns of Black women and other women of color during this time. Rather, many Black women were focusing on the right to not be sterilized, and the right to have a life and family without interference from the government and medical establishment. And around this same time, cis women and others with uteruses who were poor, disabled, incarcerated, migrant, and Indigenous were also contending with forced sterilization—and continue to face this issue today.[6]

Puerto Rican women, for instance, were used and exploited as birth-control-trial test subjects in the 1950s.

5   Here, we are referring to the classic feminist text *Our Bodies, Our Selves* by the Boston Women's Health Collective (published first in 1970), which covered a variety of DIY and alternative self-help practices for getting to know one's body and having a better understanding of one's sexual and reproductive health.

6   See Owens (2018), Roberts (1998), and Washington (2008) for more on racism within the US reproductive health care system, historically (and within feminist health movements). See https://www.nytimes.com/2020/09/29/us/ice-hysterectomies-surgeries-georgia.html for a discussion of forced hysterectomies in ICE immigrant detention centers in 2020. See Kaba (2019) and Spurgas (2021) for a discussion of violence and trauma experienced by women of color, particularly trans and gender non-conforming women of color, in the US health care and criminal systems.

Before this, Indigenous communities protested the continued, forcible removal of their children and their subsequent placement in Indian Residential Schools and state foster systems (the founder of the first of these schools, US cavalry captain Richard Henry Pratt, suggested that forced assimilation was necessary to "save" children from their own indigeneity—his words were literally "Kill the Indian in him, and save the man." The graves of children who died while in the "care" of these schools are still being unearthed across North America.) Yet, to this day, the story commonly told about the history of the reproductive rights movement is that it was a win for women at large, while the histories of broader forms of reproductive, health, family, and community self-determination have received considerably less attention. White liberal feminism at its finest! (And by "finest" we definitely mean *worst* . . .)

What is the relevance of this very brief history of community justice movements for understanding self-care today? For one thing, it's important to understand the contradictions. Even when care was meant to be radical and helpful for many folks, it didn't always (or often) work out that way. The point is not to assign blame, but to show that the *effects* of these newer movements don't always match the *intent*.

Though health activism and community- and self-care continue to be undertaken by marginalized groups as a means of collective survival, these tend to *not* be the most popular versions of "self-care" encountered today—including in online spaces (where very different—and much more commodified and lucrative—versions proliferate). Contemporary popular versions seem to have moved far afield from some previous understandings of the concept wherein structural inequality was put forth as a major cause of ill health and care was not seen as simply supplementary to social change, but rather was often the vehicle for revolutionary movement and *political* in and of itself. While current versions of self-care can and do bring needed relief for many individuals, too often elite, white, cis women, who are already privileged, are the ones to benefit most.

Moreover, contemporary self-care movements sometimes actually *further* injustice, rather than just ignoring its intersectional operations and complexities—that is: such movements can be harmful (to local communities, traditions, and the environment, among other things). Even when this is unintentional.

So: how did we get to a place where contemporary versions of self-care have become an individualist enterprise? How did "self-care" become a marketing keyword and so thoroughly commodified? How did individualist self-care come to be understood as empowering? How and why is there a multi-trillion-dollar industry surrounding wellness and self-care today? And how did self-care and its marketing come to be so firmly under the purview of elite, white, cis women in the Global North?

The Self-Care Industrial Complex: Boss Bitches to the Front!

Self-care and wellness are big business. The global wellness economy was valued at $4.9 trillion in 2019 and then fell to $4.4 trillion in 2020, due to the widespread impacts of the COVID-19 pandemic. In a (hopefully, one day) "post-pandemic" world, the wellness economy is projected to grow at 9.9 percent annually, reaching nearly $7.0 trillion in 2025. The wellness economy continues to expand faster than global economic growth.[7] To really paint this picture: in the years immediately

---

7   The data cited in this section come primarily from The
      Global Wellness Institute (GWI)'s main website https://
      globalwellnessinstitute.org/; the GWI's Global Wellness Economy
      Monitor, October 2018 https://globalwellnessinstitute.org/wp-
      content/uploads/2018/10/Research2018_v5webfinal.pdf;
      The Global Wellness Summit (GWS)'s 2018 Global Wellness
      Trends Report https://www.globalwellnesssummit.com/2018
      -global-wellness-trends/; and The Global Entrepreneurship
      Monitor (GEM)'s 2018/2019 Global Report https://www
      .gemconsortium.org/report/gem-2018-2019-global-report.

before the pandemic, the industry grew 12.8 percent and the wellness industry now represents 5.3 percent of global economic output; this is equal to more than half the size of all global health spending, which, according to data published in online tech mag *Fast Company*, was last estimated at $7.3 trillion. Today, the total valuation of the global wellness industry is bolstered in large part by the $828.2 billion "physical activity economy" (which reached $874 billion at its peak in 2019). And although this "physical activity economy" caters to both "masculine" and "feminine" tastes, many of the industry leaders and those targeted for sales in the broader wellness industry are nowadays often class-privileged, white, cis women in the Global North—or at least this demographic has secured a serious pocket within the industry.

These markets and "self-help," "wellness," and complementary and alternative medicine (CAM) more broadly are depicted, practiced, bought, and sold very differently by men and women. Some of the market sectors showing the fastest growth include:

- Personal care and beauty: $1.083 trillion
- Healthy eating, nutrition, and weight loss: $702 billion
- Wellness tourism: $639 billion
- Fitness and mind-body: $595 billion

- Preventive and personalized medicine and pub-
  lic health:[8] $575 billion
- Traditional and complementary medicine:
  $360 billion
- Wellness real estate: $134 billion
- Spa economy: $119 billion
- Thermal/mineral springs: $56 billion
- Workplace wellness: $48 billion

Women represent the majority shareholders in several of
these arenas, comprising many of the inventors, entrepreneurs, and practitioners. For example, at the invite-only
2017 Global Wellness Summit for the world's top wellness leaders, 56 percent of the delegates were women.
Women's entrepreneurial activity was up 10 percent
between 2015 and 2017, closing the gender gap by five
percent since 2014. The latest Global Entrepreneurship
Monitor (GEM) Women's Entrepreneurship Report finds
an estimated 163 million women launching new ventures
while 111 million are running established businesses.

Women entrepreneurs are 5 percent more likely
than men to be "innovative" in their businesses, including in the wellness and lifestyle markets—particularly
in North America and western Europe. In the United

---

8   We are not exactly sure what is meant here by "mind-body" or
     "public health," nor by some of the other terms in this list.

States, women are equal co-owners or majority owners of 45 percent of all privately held registered businesses, comprising 12.3 million firms. The 2018/2019 US GEM report finds that 59 percent of women entrepreneurs "perceive opportunity" for themselves, the highest rate ever recorded; though in terms of perceived startup capabilities and "fear of failure," a significant gender gap still exists.

Yet, established business ownership among women is still low around the world. In the Middle East and North Africa, which report some of the widest gender gaps, women run established businesses at one-third the rate of men. Similarly, Latin America exhibits a wide gender gap. These regions stand in contrast to North America, which reports the narrowest regional gender gap in established business activity. These gaps exist despite the fact that economies said to be in an early stage of development, such as in Sub-Saharan Africa, have the highest regional average total entrepreneurial activity (TEA) rate and strong average growth expectations, which translates into high levels of employment for women entrepreneurs.

Nevertheless, returns by women entrepreneurs tend to be lower, in part due to lower education levels, and they tend to exit their businesses more frequently due in large part to lack of support, investment, and access to capital. Here, the contrasts in region and north/south divides are laid bare. But the domination of the wellness industry by elite women in the Global North is lauded as advancing the cause of women, in general—a vulgar universalism that obscures the material differences among women depending on their location within global relationships of power and domination.

Self-care and wellness products (including those that are called "Eastern" or "Indigenous") are increasingly designed by, produced by, and bought and sold to wealthy white women. But the association of self-care with (elite, white, cis) "femininity" is more than this. These industries utilize femininity—in terms of both the *content* (what is sold) and the *form* (how it is sold)—in marketing these products, as well. E-commerce and new marketing styles and techniques change relationships between consumers, producers, and products; that is, they change *how and why people buy*. In this new "women-friendly" business world, self-care products and services are sold in an aspirational manner. Certainly, advertising has always manufactured needs and wielded aspirational content in order to drive sales (the old idiom "keeping up with the Joneses" comes to mind).

This is not new. What *is* new is that self-care products and services today are sold in an inspirational/ aspirational manner that is meant to feel like a good friend passing on ancient knowledge, or it's intended to approximate or serve as a substitute for the shared wisdom of women's communities and networks. The strategy then appears to be a "softer" and "gentler" mode of capitalism. In order to explain why these contemporary shifts in self-care are worrisome, let's first take a look at recent trends in the inequality of care.

Why Is Self-Care a Problem?

Shortly after the COVID-19 pandemic hit the United States in the spring of 2020, levels of unemployment skyrocketed, unemployed individuals lost their health care en masse, and unprecedented numbers of Americans waited in long lines at food banks, which were running out of food. All the while, the nation's billionaires substantially increased their wealth. At this point, all of this is reasonably common knowledge. What may be less well-known is that even before COVID-19, inequality in the United States was at its highest level since shortly before the Great Depression. One more time, for the people in the back: a high level of inequality in the United States is nothing new!

With that said, *for white people only*, levels of inequality dropped substantially during the mid-twentieth century. Post-war policies such as Social Security, Federal

Housing Administration-backed loans, the G.I. Bill, and urban renewal (all of which systematically excluded or negatively impacted communities of color) helped catapult many working-class white families (including ethnic white immigrants who had themselves been marginalized to varying degrees at different moments) solidly into the suburban middle-class.[9] In other words, affirmative action has always benefited white people the most! But: in the 1970s, something began to change, and things started to go downhill, economically—even for these newly middle-class white folks. That something was the result of a set of macroeconomic policies informed by a broader economic philosophy now commonly known as "neoliberalism."

We keep hearing the term "neoliberalism," but what exactly is it and what does it have to do with wellness, health, and self-care? In a nutshell, neoliberalism promotes free markets and rolling back the power of the federal government, particularly by doing the following: cutting social welfare policies (which are accused of breeding dependency and contributing to escalating federal debt), slashing or weakening regulations that are

9   On the history of these policies and their disparate impacts on white families and families of color, see Fullilove (2004) and Massey & Denton (1993).

perceived to be unfriendly to businesses (they're perfectly capable of monitoring themselves, thank you), and
cutting taxes, particularly for the wealthy and corporate
industry (a.k.a. the "job creators"). By doing all of the
above, the idea is that you free up individuals and industry to "innovate" and grow the economy. If you think
this sounds like libertarianism (or the romanticization of
"liberty"), you're not wrong.

In fact, the two philosophies are associated, because
neoliberalism is often portrayed by its advocates as promoting individual rights and freedoms. How so? Well,
without the finger-wagging of "big government" and
moreover without being grounded by the "nanny
state," the idea is that we'll all be freer to pursue our
own self-interests and make our own best rational,
common-sense decisions in the marketplace and in
society at large. And hey, if we make bad choices (life,
economic, or health decisions), then that's on us, right?
Well, maybe not if you're a big bank who, say, helped
tank the economy by engaging in (what you knew to be)
risky lending practices. In that case, it's big government
to the rescue . . . but we digress.

Needless to say, there are a lot of critiques of neoliberalism out there. Critics argue that even if these ideas
about the sanctity of freedom and rights and liberty were

sound, industry has a vested interest in hiding information from the public that would help us make informed economic decisions (this is known as an "information asymmetry"). Perhaps even more importantly, the reality of entrenched inequality means that we are not all equally positioned to make rational, common-sense decisions in the marketplace based on our own self-interest, regardless of how much high-quality information we might have! Further, by gutting social safety nets and promoting free market solutions to social and economic problems, the most marginalized among us fall deeper into poverty and ill health. And finally, by emphasizing personal responsibility over any other factor, individuals and communities that "fail" to make "optimal" and "rational" marketplace and health decisions get blamed as irresponsible at best or, at worst, as "takers not makers" (this racist and classist dog whistle brought to you by the former dynamic duo Mitt Romney and Paul Ryan, who ran for US president and vice president in 2012 on the Republican ticket).

Of course it sounds bad when we put it like that, but the really wild thing is that rather than seeing the promotion of individual responsibility for both health outcomes and life chances as an artful dodge on the part of politicians, industry, and employers, large numbers of us—across the political spectrum—have instead inter-nalized these ideas as "common sense," and in some cases, as *empowering*. That is, by acting prudently, responsibly, preemptively, and even speculatively, we presume that we might avoid future risk by making lifestyle changes *now*. And for many of us, that feels like that most holy of rights: personal freedom. It feels healthy and like *self-care*! In effect, under neoliberalism, we each become our own personal CEO—reducing risk and optimizing capacity through our own self-entrepreneurial market-place decisions.

The core ideals of neoliberalism have a deep basis in the (white) American Protestant work ethic and cul-tural values, as well as in broader economic and (racist, sexist, homophobic, etc.) social concerns. In the 1970s, both the economy and average incomes were stagnating, manufacturing jobs were disappearing, the social wel-fare state was under attack, the power of labor unions was declining, employers were shifting a greater share of the burden for escalating health costs onto employees, and public hospitals were closing. Things were a mess. Even middle-class white Americans no longer felt con-fident that they and their children would continue to benefit from a rising standard of living as they had for much of the twentieth century.

So, working to improve one's self—and, especially, one's *health*—became a means by which to address larger anxieties about the changing nature of modern life and one's (potentially precarious) position within it.[10] That is, taking personal responsibility became a way to regain a sense of control. By the 1980s, this type of neoliberal thinking was deeply entrenched: Americans began to think of themselves quite readily as "consumers" of their own health care and as in charge of their own health destinies.

During this same period of time, the American public was also becoming disillusioned with the power of medicine to adequately address chronic disease, while published medical research began emphasizing the connection between lifestyle behaviors and health outcomes. "Exercise more and eat less fat!" was the new self-help health mantra (No, wait: eat fewer carbs. No, wait: . . . ?!). Continuing a trend begun in the 1960s, middle-class white Americans increasingly turned to complementary and alternative medicine (CAM) for health solutions. As documented by health and medicine scholar Michael Goldstein (2002), within CAM, the focus is less on

10 For a full elaboration of this history of "healthism" and the "medicalization of everyday life" see the work of medical sociologist Robert Crawford.

addressing disease and more on working toward the goal of achieving "holistic" health. Individuals, working with practitioners as facilitators of this process, carefully monitor the body's signs and symptoms, seeking to understand them and how they can be addressed.

While CAM's growth in popularity in the 1970s and 1980s was linked to the collective care practices of earlier social movements and was a response to growing disillusionment with standard medicine, an emphasis on personal responsibility for health was woven throughout the field. In this sense, though CAM has often been associated with progressivism, it has ultimately served the ideals of neoliberalism. How so? Consider, as an example, the self-help mogul Louise Hay, who argued that "positive affirmations" heal the body and mind whereas "negative self-talk" and emotions bring on disease. Hay literally suggested that lingering resentments over sexual abuse and rape lead to cervical cancer, including her own! The "power of positive thinking" was the reigning doctrine, and in many cases, it was taken to an extreme . . .

There are a few points worth expanding on in terms of the relationship between self-care, health practices, and neoliberalism. First, given that people are constantly bombarded with information about new forms of risk that we must constantly guard against, *health* has become an ever-receding horizon, more and more difficult to fully inhabit or attain. We are all expected to constantly work at it through acts of self-help and *self-care*, and because of this, health has become a preoccupation for many, particularly among the middle-class and wealthy.

Second, by focusing on individuals themselves as both the cause of and remedy for ill health, alternative wellness, self-help, and self-care movements obscure the broader social, political, and economic determinants of health outcomes, disparities, and behaviors. Quite simply, these DIY movements are so shrouded in individualism that they hide the structural causes of health inequities. In this sense, these forms of care are entirely compatible with the perpetuation of existing systems of disempowerment and inequality, despite their progressive veneer.

Finally, by creating health as a "super value," alternative wellness, self-help, and self-care movements sometimes actually *advance* health inequality in two ways. The continual self-monitoring and self-improvement require time, energy, and resources—all of which are, of course, less available to low-income and other marginalized groups. And neoliberal portrayals of health (including those found in CAM) attach great meaning, virtue, and morality to health—the assumption that each of us has a personal responsibility to restore/optimize our own health is known as "healthism." Thus, anyone not adequately on the track to self-improvement and health-enhancement is viewed as lazy and irresponsible. This brings us back full circle to the contemporary versions of self-care and self-care markets we examine throughout this book.

"But Seriously, We Like Yoga and Gluten-Free Food!"

As with previous iterations of middle-class wellness efforts, contemporary self-care practices proliferate in a larger context of cultural anxiety and social, political, and economic precarity. Beyond record levels of economic inequality, the last decade (and especially the last few years since the 2016 US presidential election) has been fraught with crises. Even if we just take the US as a case study, the nation is polarized and ridden with strife.

High numbers of individuals report disillusionment with government, as well as growing distrust in science and institutions of higher education.

Health researchers have suggested we are in the midst of a "loneliness epidemic."

Climate change is ever-present in the news and what it has wrought and continues to wretch upon the planet is plainly obvious (though some continue to deny its existence).

And beginning in early 2020, we have had to contend with a global pandemic, the likes of which has not been seen in a century since the influenza pandemic of 1918. This was all on top of the Donald Trump presidency, which certainly called for its own regimes of self-care (or self-medication/intoxication. Or all of the above.).[11]

It's no wonder, then, that initial data suggest that anxiety levels have recently risen in all age groups, notably more so in women than men and amongst Black and Latinx individuals more so than whites. And the American Psychiatric Association recently found that the top reasons people report that they are "somewhat anxious" to "extremely anxious" include lack of family safety, health, and economic security.

---

11   Of note: we drafted this book on the cusp of the 2020 US presidential election, in which the catastrophe of four years under Donald Trump had been laid bare, and the country was about to choose whether or not to re-elect him. It is possible that the collective anxiety—and, thus, the need for care—had never felt so pronounced at any point in our lives. This feeling has continued but taken new forms since that time, particularly as COVID-19 variants surge in the face of abject systemic failure to adequately respond to the pandemic, domestically and internationally.

And so, there are—of course—very legitimate reasons why, during these increasingly uncertain and brutal times, people need self-care. This is not our quarrel.

Social media apps and other online forums, for instance, are key places where individuals learn about and share tips, tricks, and products for self-care, and so these spaces may provide a sense of solace and community. Yet, most current versions of self-care encourage individuals (particularly those who are already relatively advantaged) to manage risk and uncertainty by taking personal control of their health and well-being to better withstand hardship and moreover to *succeed*—even in debilitating circumstances of political, economic, and social precarity and austerity. This is the great irony—the very things which have caused the need for care in the first place become the guiding framework for how to solve the problem (on your own!). These regimes of self-care rarely advocate collective action alongside individual efforts to provide relief (that is, beyond virtue signaling and hashtag profiteering, the quintessential characteristics of our newest phase of self-care—which we will have much more to say about as we go on, don't you worry . . .). And in neglecting this crucial *collective* aspect, these regimes and commodities too often reproduce the very forces, relations, and systems that drive current crises.

★ ★ ★

Please keep in mind that throughout this book, we will poke fun at some things that many readers may really enjoy and find great utility in. We do this with the full knowledge of how contradictory we all are as human beings. After all, we like these things, too! And we actually do think it's possible to enjoy gluten-free and organic products, and engage in mindfulness practices and yoga, while also critiquing how the self-care industry operates on a broad scale. As North American sociologists who are, demographically speaking, more similar to the promoters and beneficiaries of the self-care marketplaces that we critique than not, we live with these contradictions (seriously: one of us is a certified yoga instructor and the other could start a small library with the CAM books already on her shelves). And we should make it clear that we know that self-care markets, self-care promoters, and self-care profiteers—not to mention scientists, clinicians, researchers, and other "experts"—are of course far more complex than we can fully attend to in this book. Rather than spending time unpacking all that complexity, we want to highlight the broad picture of self-care, alternative wellness, and lifestyle enhancement that comes into focus when all of the trends we describe here network together.

To this end, we don't intend this book to be a call-out of specific individuals who profit from self-care markets (though we do think it's important to broadly name what *types* of people benefit most). Rather than suggest the problem lies with the behaviors or motivations of individual actors, we focus in on the larger systems which shape the beliefs and practices of communities, groups, populations, and public cultures (rewarding or inhibiting them in one direction or the other), in the first place. Specifically, we examine the definitions, meanings, assumptions, and values of contemporary versions of self-care, as described in key published texts, and situate them within the larger context of structural inequality (read: under racial capitalism and colonialism). Herein, we are guided by the decolonizing work of scholars, activists, and scholar-activists who have been at the forefront for movements for change and justice.

From a decolonizing perspective, self-care and wellness more broadly are not things that can be bought or sold by individuals in an attempt to withstand, let alone thrive under, increasingly toxic social, political, economic, and ecological environments. Rather, *care* is an inseparable part of collectively dismantling and transforming these toxic environments. Herein, as Tuck and Yang among so many other decolonial activists make clear, decoloniality is a praxis rather than an endpoint. Individuals collectively and iteratively dream up, build, and live alternatives to the contemporary colonial order, connecting, changing, and growing along the way.

Gender, sexuality, eating, and functional medicine are analyzed here as key sites of "improvement" in contemporary self-care movements—realms wherein many of the individualistic and neoliberal phenomena we have just outlined are on full display. In Chapter 2, we discuss mindfulness, tantra, and other trends in sexual enhancement as these are targeted to and taken up by women in the Global North. In Chapter 3, we tackle gendered "extreme" travel, biohacking, and other forms of "fem-tech"—again, with an eye toward how these new "softer," "gentler" markets are designed by and for women (with a very specific—that is: wealthy, white, cis, straight—femininity in mind). In Chapter 4, we examine how advocates of gluten-free and low-carb (GFLC) diets and functional medicine approach causes of and remedies for various illnesses. While proponents in these domains may occasionally highlight broader structural factors such as the nature of the food system or the profit motivations of the health insurance industry (which are important!), ultimately, the locus of change in all of these areas tends to remain firmly at the level of the individual.

In ending this book, we highlight the newest moment of self-care: a form that has taken shape based on (too often hollow) calls for "diversity," "equity," and "inclusion." We make clear why simply diversifying existing forms of self-care is *not* the way forward, and instead reflects just another iteration of neoliberal or protocol feminism—a "feminism" that centers whiteness. This newest phase of self-care in fact makes "being woke" and "invested in the community"—or even the very notion of being politically aware at all—*trendy* and *cool*. But, most often, these caring investments *beyond the self* are ultimately framed as good because they are *good for the self* (including one's own mental and physical health). By contrast, we attempt to think through and put forward caring alternatives to these forms of neoliberal and neocolonial self-care.

We do not offer any easy answers, nor do we offer universal truths. Instead of articulating our own spelled-out crystal-clear vision, we highlight contemporary forms of organizing that are instituting alternative ways of providing care. As with activists in the mid-late twentieth century, these movements are putting in place practices and parallel structures that support self-community-earth as part of the process of working to dismantle the existing toxic material and social order. We draw inspiration from these groups and movements, and we hope that you will, too.

Chapter 1

HOW TO HAVE AMAZING SEX [AND BECOME YOUR BEST SELF IN THE PROCESS]: HARNESS YOUR RECEPTIVE FEMININITY AND PRACTICE MINDFULNESS!

In 2013, a group of Scotland-based researchers provided evidence for what many had already believed for a very long time: Women are better than men at multi-tasking. Since then, other studies have offered support for gender similarity in multi-tasking, but what we are interested in is how much attention and traction this particular study received. The researchers raise the question: is it actually a good thing to multi-task? How useful is it? Since this study was published and widely cited, the negative effects of doing too many things at once, and suggestions for preventing these deleterious consequences, have been emphasized even more.

In fact, evolutionary psychologists have been claiming for quite a while that the first multi-taskers were women. Many say that women are inherently better at multi-tasking—that multi-tasking is a feminine trait. Some suggest this is due to hardwiring from cavepeople times, when women had to juggle the multiple responsibilities of caring for babies, keeping an eye out for predators, and gathering things (like berries? children? rocks, aka the children's toys?). In an interview for *National Geographic* about the Scottish 2013 study, when asked why women are better at multi-tasking, the lead author states: " . . . we were essentially adapted to surviving the dangers of a Stone Age environment. In that environment women did more than look after their children. They could not just focus on making clothes or finding food. At the same time, they had to keep an eye on their children; if not, the children would have been eaten by wild animals and the race would have died out. We are the result of that successful behavior."[12]

Although plenty of claims have been made about the "adaptive" or "evolved" reasons women became so adept at juggling multiple tasks at once, we would like to suggest that there is really no need to look to evolutionary psychology speculation to explain this phenomenon. Plenty of contemporary analyses of work, care, and self-care have examined multi-tasking and its gendered origins and (negative) effects.

More recently, in the twentieth century A.D., for instance, and particularly during the economic boom of the post-World-War-II United States, the so-called private and public spheres were instituted as separate. The *public* became associated with the world of "work," "politics," and "production" and the *private* was associated

12   Deluca (2013).

with "intimacy," "domesticity," and "reproduction." In effect, The Public became the world of men and The Private the world of women[13]—and the responsibilities in these two places were very different. The divide in spheres further heralded a gender division in labor and *recovery* from that labor—and the types of work that happened in the private sphere were imagined to require specific forms of preparation and after-care (ultimately *self*-care) for women.

One potential resulting malady was purportedly due to multi-tasking itself—which, as necessary as it was within the cult of domesticity, might also hinder a woman's sexual desire. This unfortunate side effect was one that she would of course need to attend to—and the connection between multi-tasking, stress, distractibility, and low desire for women is a common theme in discussions of self-care and self-help today (which are, notably, rife with discussions of sex as a form of self-care). Before we get to self-care and desire enhancement, however, it's important to consider how multi-tasking was wedded to

---

13 The work of women of color has always exploded this binary and is explored throughout this book—here, we want to examine the neoliberal imperatives implemented via the *logic* of this "public/private" divide, even as we know it was actually instituted for only a brief time historically, was very geographically specific, and certainly did not fit with most people's lived experiences.

household management, home economics, and domestic hygiene, and how housework itself became a "calling" for (white) women—and possibly even the first example of a personal or lifestyle brand.

Housewives, Optimizing: The Origins of Mindfulness for Ultimate Productivity

In most discussions of how the two different spheres operated, scientific management or Taylorism was associated with the public sphere or what happens in the factory or on the shop floor.

Workers could be made more productive if their movements were measured—how many moves did it take to assemble the thing on the factory line?

How many strokes of the typewriter were required to finish the document?

How quickly and efficiently could any given industrialized task be completed?

The Taylorist workplace of scientific management was a space (even before the Fordist automobile assembly line), where automation—and *optimization* or *enhancement*—were key. If the manager could figure out how long it *ought* to take to do a certain task, then he could make sure all workers were being held to that standard. Further, workers' own times could be compared—workers were encouraged to beat their *own* records, ensuring they remain on the path to being their "best selves."

This logic of comparing workers against each other in the name of efficiency, and even comparing workers against themselves, was, of course, inherently ableist—insofar as it created an ideal and forced a normative mode of embodiment and behavior on human beings in the name of productivity. It is important to note that this theme continues in the self-help, self-optimization, "be-your-best-self" neoliberal wellness sphere today—with racist, sexist, ableist, classist, and nationalist consequences.

Importantly, alongside what was happening in that public work world, other folks (usually the ones we call women) were doing the reproductive work in the private, "intimate" world of the home. And they didn't have specialized tasks assigned to them within a Fordist or bureaucratic setting; they had to create their own. Middle-class white housewives became the managers of the *household*—their job was to hierarchize tasks that needed completing in the home, and to delegate the ones they couldn't complete themselves.

In her 2018 book *Counterproductive: Time Management in the Knowledge Economy*, social theorist and tech researcher Melissa Gregg describes how early-twentieth-century white housewives were both managers and

workers who needed to keep pace, multi-task, and track
the happenings in the home. Some folks tend to think
of this type of multi-tasking as a more contemporary
phenomenon—it's what we are consumed with in *platform* or *cognitive* capitalism (an economy and society that
is built by software engineers and which is increasingly
decentralized), particularly as so many jobs are online,
and operate according to the mandates of "just-in-time"
management strategies and the ever-expanding gig or
"sharing" economy. But the point here is that an obses-
sion with multi-tasking—and marking it as something
feminine—is not a new phenomenon (nor is it evolutionarily ordained).

Gregg makes a convincing case that housewives
have, in the words of the popular writer Jia Tolentino,
"always be[en] optimizing." Housewives of the 1950s
were the original managerial class. Of course, we hear
less about the roles that poor women, disabled and trans
women, and women of color played in the delegation
scheme. These marginalized women were integral parts
of the reproduction process (of home and daily life)—
and they often *had* to multitask in a more covert and,
simultaneously, life-or-death fashion, as they cared for
monied white women's children and families in addition to their own. So there are, in fact, two levels to
the hidden intimate or domestic management of the

early twentieth century, beyond men in blue-collar factories and later in white-collar offices—there were the white women supporting their men, and Black and Brown women keeping the whole show running behind the scenes.

Even so, the running of a good home, on an efficient schedule, was suggested to be something the white middle-class housewife uniquely possessed the ability to do well—hence the common sense perception, sometimes framed in evolutionary terms, of women's inherent ability to multi-task. And being a good manager was not only indicative of the housewife's own "calling" and her goodness *as a woman*, her managerial skills provided the structural support for the nation. A hospitable, organized, and well-run home (by a graceful, pious, and convivial woman—this part was imperative!) was part and parcel of "euthenics." The sister to eugenics, euthenics was the original form of home economics—less about breeding the perfect individual, and more about breeding *the perfect environment in which he would thrive*. As it was ultimately meant to support the perpetuation of the most evolved members of "the human race," euthenics was an inherently colonialist, white supremacist, classist, ableist, and nationalist enterprise.

Importantly, feminized multitasking managers had to get ready—and recharge. Housewives were encouraged to take a moment before beginning their day to spiritually prepare themselves for the tasks at hand. This moment was to be dedicated to solitary reflection, an uninterrupted time to prioritize daily duties, but it was also intended to be a centering and grounding experience. That this meditative experience would aid their efficiency made the "gathering moment" worthwhile. In the post-secular, early-mid-twentieth-century United States, the maintaining of an orderly home became *its own calling*, and the management of the home became its own quasi-spiritual experience.

And, of course, the work should be done with a smile.

The first thing to note is that through this description of "women's work" we begin to see how productivity becomes a calling in and of itself. No longer part of an explicitly Protestant ethic, work was becoming spiritual, its own kind of special fulfillment. Within this dynamic, the white bourgeois housewife merges the public and private, brings work and play together, creates *and feels fulfilled by creating* her own *brand*.

Work became a lifestyle. Work was everything—a means *and* an end. And cleanliness was most certainly next to godliness. Hence, we see the beginning of white women's tasking as middle management, with aspirational goals for "getting ahead"—and this was work they often did very much take on, in the name of their men, their families, and the nation, but also for their own benefit. This was the work of white liberal feminism in its nascent stages.

The second thing of note here is that as work became more and more routinized, and there was less and less "time off," *self-care* became imperative in the face of the drudgery of decentralized precarious finance capitalism. But even in the earlier moments of capitalism, we have a predecessor to this; it was imperative for the housewife to have "down time," to take time off to care for herself—so she could adequately and selflessly take care of others. Although we see this self-care rhetoric applied across working populations today, it is still the case that those who have historically been *understood* as social reproducers (wealthy or middle-class, white, cis women) *and* those who have historically actually *done* the bulk of the back-breaking reproductive work (poor and working-class women, immigrants, and women of color) both seem to need or want self-care the most. So this is where we are at today—the bizarre juxtaposition: self-care as radical, communal, and absolutely necessary within marginalized communities, right next to self-care markets and entire multi-trillion-dollar

industries designed for the feminized elite. We also
arrive fully at (even though we kind of had it before
with the "gathering moment") *mindfulness*. Mindfulness
literally and truly everywhere—the perfect individualized cure-all for everything that ails us and the way to
make us *better*.

Apparently, Ericka Huggins and Angela Davis did
yoga, meditated, and maybe even practiced mindfulness—while leading the Black radical revolution,
including while in prison. Sometimes, folks who are
traumatized, mistreated, and worked to the bone do
benefit from these practices. But while some see a caring, communal, anti-capitalist potential in mindfulness,
meditation, and the broad taking-up of "loving kind-
ness"—including on the job—we have our doubts.[14] Is
it possible for mindfulness to be utilized in a collectivist, revolutionary way, as a real rupture or break from

14 Some have celebrated employer-promoted mindfulness
    and meditation regimens, gig/sharing economy "live/work
    spaces," and sober morning pre-work dance parties such
    as "Daybreakers" (often with major corporate "wellness"
    sponsors) as offering real change to the world of monotonous
    and alienated work (see Gregg 2018 for a discussion). We do
    not feel that these offer very much in the way of radical or
    revolutionary possibility, as they have become so seamlessly
    integrated into the fabric of late neoliberal capitalism and seem
    intended primarily to help workers *cope*.

capitalism? Or is it really just a way to prepare us to work even harder, next time?

DIY Medicine, Every Day, All the Time: Self-Control & the Contradictions of 24/7 Mindfulness

Mindfulness discourse is riddled with contradictions, first and foremost being its simultaneous emphasis on *acceptance* of ill health states, situated right next to the language and goals of not only healing but *cure*.

The core tenets of mindfulness in the Buddhist tradition would suggest that ill people should accept their situations in order to mitigate suffering and let their negative feelings about their experiences pass, that they should observe them without judgment. But the most popular medical mindfulness texts often relay stories of those who have "overcome" their illnesses (or, even more egregiously, who have "optimized" and "enhanced" their physical health, mental acuity, sexual desire, and more!)—which sends some very ambivalent and ambiguous messages. There is a good deal of confusion as to what the ultimate goal of mindfulness is in terms of *care* versus *cure* here.

In a lot of mindfulness talk, there is also a simultaneous push and pull in relation to institutionalized medicine. Medical sociologist Kristin Barker argues that although mindfulness is suggested as an alternative to orthodox medicine, in many ways it solidifies the power of medicine and the ever-expanding nature of *medicalization* (i.e., thinking of and attending to ourselves through a medical lens, including via self-diagnosis and self-treatment) as a form of self-optimization—but just re-packages the whole thing as part of the "do-it-yourself" or "DIY" movement.

The DIY idea is this: now we can practice medicalization at literally every moment via mindfulness, on our own, as everyday life here is also increasingly framed as pathological, stress-inducing, and in need of *working on*. That is: in the world of commodified mindfulness, what is considered pathological or in need of treatment/improvement, in everyday life, is (paradoxically) expanded.

"Traditional" practitioners are increasingly taking up mindfulness in their medical practices, as well, which indicates that mindfulness is becoming more and more mainstream (and this is also clear from examining the broad reach of Jon Kabat-Zinn's protocol into mainstream medical spaces, to be examined more in a moment). This turn to DIY complementary and alternative medicine is often based on fears, concerns, and disillusionment over the so-called "modern condition." But: we would like to emphasize the fact that white people feeling jaded does *not* justify cultural appropriation and neocolonialism!—particularly the very real material aspects of these and the harms they cause.

Another strange mindfulness contradiction is in the framing of "stress" as a key factor determining pathology and illness—in the most popular mindfulness texts, the social and external world are often referred to *as inherently stressful*; this is particularly the case in the modern context of late capitalism, in which we are all understood to be overwhelmed with hyper-connectivity, technology overloads, perpetual work, and too much multi-tasking (as we have mentioned, this problem of "too much multi-tasking" appears to be particularly bad for "the modern woman," whose sexual desire may even be dampened as a consequence!).

However, mindfulness devotees proceed with the idea that their physical and mental health is really *under their own control*. So there is also an insidious victim-blaming, pull-yourself-by-your-own-bootstraps mentality that is entirely compatible with the mandates of neoliberal self-improvement—even as the world is framed as *so damn stressful*, if stress is getting the best of you (and there is rarely a social analysis of the highly unequal distribution of "stress" via race, class, and gender in popular mindfulness rhetoric), then *do something about it*! Your fate is in your own hands.

The emphasis on a strong and "healthy" mind-body connection also makes the need for mindfulness even clearer: because mindfulness practitioners presume that physical health is so heavily influenced by "positive" vs. "negative" attitude, then we can all ultimately control how sick or healthy we are (or how much we're optimizing) even in the face of terrible things that might happen to us in the world, unequally—like how people of color and poor people and trans folks and women (especially when they are in more than one of these categories at once) literally experience way more stressors and daily traumas in their lives than more privileged folks. But hell, having a positive attitude and being mindful might even be enough to change a person's biological predispositions, according to this logic! Barker puts it best: "albeit in different ways, both orthodox medicine and mindfulness overemphasize the individual and underemphasize the social."[15]

Mindfulness & Sexual Well-Being: "Potent," "Sensual," and "Feminine" Women, "Tuning In"

Within neoliberal medicine and health enhancement in the Global North, mindfulness—concisely, non-judgmentally staying present with negative emotions and affects and "letting them pass"—first began to

15   Barker (2014), p. 174.

widely appear in the late 1970s, when Jon Kabat-Zinn founded his Stress Reduction Clinic at the University of Massachusetts Medical School. Kabat-Zinn, an MIT-trained molecular biologist and anti-war activist from New York City, had become interested in mindfulness and meditation through his work with Zen missionaries and after reading the work of (and eventually training with) Buddhist mindfulness practitioners such as Thích Nhất Hạnh. Kabat-Zinn later named his structured eight-week course Mindfulness-Based Stress Reduction (MBSR). And so began the full inclusion of mindfulness within the contemporary scientific and medical context.

Today, Kabat-Zinn's books, including his first, *Full Catastrophe Living: Using the Wisdom of Your Body and Mind to Face Stress, Pain, and Illness*,[16] published in 1990, are still bestsellers on the subject of mindfulness. On a list of the "Top 50 Best Mindfulness Books" for positivepsychology.com from January 2020, Kabat-Zinn's books have their own section, as "he has been a major

16   Curiously, the original title of this book was *Full Catastrophe Living: How to Cope with Stress, Pain and Illness Using Mindfulness Meditation*. We have not been able to find an explanation for why the word "cope" was removed from the title, and in some versions, the word still appears today—but it seems to suggest that the author (or his publisher) realized that the word "cope" carried a negative connotation.

figure in popularizing mindfulness teachings in the West, and he's written too many valuable books to pick just one for this list." Not only are Kabat-Zinn's westernized mindfulness teachings mainstays of complementary and alternative medicine and healing today, they have also taken root in a variety of more orthodox medical institutions. Thus, they suggest the contemporary crossover between more traditional medicine and the alternative avenues. For instance, the ideas Kabat-Zinn put forward regarding mindfulness and stress reduction have been taken up in medical programs for the treatment of everything from chronic pain to anxiety and depression to borderline personality disorder to female sexual dysfunction and low desire.

In psychology, mindfulness is generally considered the "third wave" of behavioral therapy—it is often used in conjunction with cognitive behavioral therapy or CBT (hence when mindfulness is included, it is sometimes called "MCBT"). The idea behind CBT is that you can change your own patterns of thought, leading to an alteration of behavior and a better quality of life—this is the mainstay of psychological intervention today, since it (along with psychopharmacology) replaced psychoanalytic therapies in the latter half of the twentieth century.

But: westernized mindfulness, based on non-judgment and letting negative thoughts pass *without* trying to change them, sits uneasily within behavioral medicine and its emphasis on cognitive restructuring and behavior modification. It sits uneasily alongside CBT. Given this troubled juxtaposition, it should be unsurprising that mindfulness is often ultimately used in a more goal-oriented way than it was originally intended, and as a means to a rationalized end (that is: toward behavior change and modification of the self, life, and identity). Pop psychology's interest in mindfulness is often paired with work on "flow" states, and now "mindfulness," "flow," and "being in the present," along with "attention" and even the Buddhist phrase "loving-kindness," have all become key terms in the complementary and alternative medicine (CAM) sphere over the last thirty years. It is not a stretch to say that mindfulness has been poised as a type of panacea for the work-worn, over-stimulated, and disconnected—and as perhaps especially helpful for those distracted and stretched-too-thin (lady) multi-taskers.

At the turn of the twenty-first century, mindfulness became an integral part of any decent self-care regimen—positioned as what would help us all keep our sanity (and, perhaps paradoxically, stay on task . . .). And, insofar as regularly having sex has also been linked to overall health and well-being, mindfulness was increasingly utilized toward the goal of desire augmentation and sexual enhancement—and, most often, it was targeted to (straight, cis—and, of course, low-desiring) women.

A combination of mindfulness, desire enrichment, and sexual optimization, brought together in a program for women's empowerment and self-care, ascended as the winning formula for today's frenzied female.

Originally used in the sexual health context to treat pain resulting from gynecologic surgeries, mindfulness is now applied widely to the treatment of low desire—and for the last more than twenty years, since the inception of the protocol, has been geared primarily toward cisgender women. In an interview with Vancouver-based founding foremother of mindful sex, Lori Brotto, in *The New York Times Magazine* in 2009, journalist Daniel Bergner relays the following about the birth of mindfulness-based sex therapy (MBST) as a treatment for women's low desire:

> One day at yoga class, Brotto tried the combination [mindfulness plus cognitive behavioral restructuring]. She went through her usual yoga poses, but with "a cognitive reframe" . . . she told herself, "over and over like a mantra," that she was an especially sexual woman, "capable of a high level of desire, a high level of response." And, she recalled, "there was

a deliberate intent not only to listen to my body even
more than I normally would in yoga but also to *interpret the signs from my body as signs of my sexual identity*"
[italics added].

Given this account from a licensed medical practitioner
who is also one of the most prominent, respected, and
well-known sex therapists and sex researchers today
(just google "mindfulness," "women," and "desire" and
she will be your first hit), the application of mindfulness
and CBT methodology to desire enhancement is particularly important to examine.

Mindful sex is one avenue within both the more traditional medical arena and within complementary and
alternative medicine (CAM) that is consistently getting
more and more attention. Right next to mindful eating,
drinking, and parenting, mindful sexuality is becoming
a keyword of our times. So not only is mindfulness discourse ubiquitous, but it is regularly linked to enhancing
desire and becoming your "best *sexual* self"—for your
own health, pleasure, and happiness. It is readily available
in the form of medicalized, scientific, and more reputable
or legitimate versions, including with its application via the
aforementioned mindfulness-based sex therapy (MBST)
and other health education tools, right alongside pop
self-help versions on all manner of internet media—some
of which seem to be rarely vetted by clinicians or scientists.

But these poles (clinical medicine vs. internet self-help) are increasingly collapsing. Thus, somewhat paradoxically, mindfulness represents both a shift away from dominant medical orthodoxy, and simultaneously a shift *toward* an even more overdetermined and ubiquitous institutionalization of (alternative) medicine. Mindfulness has become the crossover or bridge between snake oil and Goop, on the one hand, and legitimate scientific research and clinical therapies, on the other.

Although mindfulness is often framed as gender-, race-, and class-neutral (i.e., "mindfulness is for everyone!"), many of its practical instantiations (including those derived from the earliest westernized texts, such as those of Kabat-Zinn) are targeted to cis women. Beyond this targeting, mindfulness itself, and how it is to be used with the best effects, is in fact often framed as gender specific. And this is particularly true in the realm of sexual well-being, where a whitewashed "evolutionary" gender binary is regularly shored up, and even more often, simply taken for granted as assumed background knowledge.

All of this has too often translated into the simplistic formula: "men = high/active desire + women = low/receptive desire." And mindfulness programs have been designed to cater to each side of this (white, straight, bourgeois) gender equation.

A representative popular case study here is mindful sex and tantra guru Diana Richardson's TED talk, "The Power of Mindful Sex," recorded in 2018. The talk has received, at the time of this writing, over 800,000 views on YouTube since it was uploaded that year, continues to receive many hits, and has logged hundreds of watchers' and subscribers' comments—most of which are glowing and laudatory. Richardson, who is renowned for authoring several best-selling books on mindfulness and sexuality, discusses mindful sex as a contrast to the "goal-oriented" sex she says most people are fixated on. She discusses how couples might apply the principles of mindfulness, meditation, and tantra to their love lives, acknowledging that most of her sex therapy work has been with cisgender heterosexual pairs (she doesn't use those terms, however).

Although Richardson states that mindfulness can be applied to sex for all couples, across sexualities and genders, her framework is undeniably focused on straight cis men and women, and she frequently calls up the differences in "masculine" and "feminine" orientations to sex and sexuality in her talk. This discussion is not only reductive in its framing of masculinity and femininity, but the terms applied are also, at their core, deeply western and white. Of note is that the "feminine" side of the gender binary has historically been associated specifically with *white* women[17]—who were most often framed as sexually receptive or passive (unlike women of color, especially Black women, who were more likely to be framed as asexual and/or without gender, and in some cases, as sexually aggressive or hypersexual).

Richardson conjures "receptive femininity," also a key term in contemporary scientific and clinical studies of female sexuality (more on that in a bit), when articulating nine basic principles for applying mindfulness to sexuality. In discussing the importance of setting aside time for sex—"make a date, set aside two to three hours or more of undisturbed time"—she states:

> This works very well for women, because the female body warms up and opens up to sex much more slowly than the male body . . . when the female body is open and ready, this will completely raise the quality of the exchange for both [partners] . . . and for men, having a date is very helpful because men are often walking around wondering when they will next be able to have sex again [audience laughs, along with Richardson] . . . for sure! . . . if he knows

17   For an in-depth discussion of the gender binary as embedded in western, white settler colonialism and racist science, see Hartman (1997); Lugones (2007, 2010); Maldonado-Torres (2016); Markowitz (2001); McWhorter (2004, 2009); Snorton (2017); Somerville (1994, 2000); Spillers (1987); Tlostanova & Mignolo (2012).

that it's going to happen tomorrow night, or tonight, then he's much more relaxed, present, centered with himself—and with *you*! ["you" being the cis woman partner in the tacitly cisgender-heterosexual or cis-het couple.]

It is in her final comment that the gender stereotypes embedded in this sex therapy framework come through the most clearly—building a mindful sex practice is obviously for women. The takeaway here is that men would be okay without doing this, but women *need* it. And when women are happy, then men will be happier, too! (We assume because they won't be nagged as much by their annoying female partners?)

The fact that everyone in this equation is cis, straight, and inclined to engage in penetrative penile-vaginal intercourse is at the very least implicit, and at times, it is made explicit—throughout the rest of her discussion of the basic tenets of mindful sex, Richardson also mentions the importance of slowing down during entrance (umm), being aware and mindful upon each moment of insertion, and of using adequate lubrication. That this mindful sex is cis-het and penetrative is pretty clear.

Richardson ends the talk with: "I am here . . . to share with you a life-changing truth, that awareness in sex creates love, generates love, and nurtures connection . . . let us begin the true sexual revolution, and create a new experience for humanity—a world where couples live in harmony, where sex improves the longer you are together, where sex brings healing, connection, confidence, clarity . . . where sex invites love and peace on earth." Mindfulness here is not only targeted to elite white women, but it is meant to heal them, to heal their relationships and families, and possibly to heal the institution of heterosexuality itself.[18] Mindful sex might save the damn planet!

When a popular "crossover" talk such as Richardson's[19] is considered within the world of mindful sex more broadly—from women's magazines, podcasts, and other online self-help media sources to, perhaps most

18 See Spurgas (2020) and Ward (2020) for recent critiques of the gendered work of heterosexuality.

19 Unlike Brotto, who is a respected researcher and a licensed sex therapist, it is unclear exactly what Richardson's credentials are (besides a law degree?), and the same goes for many others in the popular mindful sex sphere. Another example of the pop version is the work of actress cum mindful sex teacher Jessica Graham, author of *Good Sex: Getting Off Without Checking Out* (2017), who has been featured on multiple podcasts, including the very popular "Multiamory" podcast, "Together," and "The Embodiment Podcast." And recently, Brotto herself has entered the popular self-help domain, publishing *Better Sex Through Mindfulness: How Women Can Cultivate Desire* (2018), a pop bestseller targeted to (cis women) lay readers to help them enhance their desire, and being featured on the 2022 Netflix docuseries *The Principles of Pleasure*.

importantly, the scientific research that provides the backbone for all of this (and within the popular genre, some pieces are authored by clinicians and researchers themselves, or these pieces at least reference their work)—the white and cis-heteronormative gender stereotypes surrounding mindful sex become apparent.

In fact, entire research, clinical, and therapeutic industries have developed since the turn of the twenty-first century, in which mindfulness began to be regularly applied within sex therapy settings. And, as mentioned, studies conducted on the "effectiveness" of mindful sex have (up until very recently) almost entirely focused on cis women, in large part due to related scientific frameworks that configure female sexuality as responsive, receptive, and *discordant* (that is: there is a perceived frequent disconnect or disjuncture between a [most often straight] woman's *subjective desire* [the low-desiring mind] and her *objective physiological arousal* [the always-already-aroused body]).[20] The naturalization of responsive, receptive, and discordant feminine desire

20 See the work of Ellen Laan and Meredith Chivers for some of the most widely disseminated research on female discordance; for a particularly prominent example, see Chivers, et al. (2010). See Basson (2000) for the foundational discussion of women's "responsive" or "circular" desire. For critiques of this "feminized responsive desire framework," see Spurgas (2020).

make it ripe for treatment—or is it management?—via mindfulness.

Longtime British mindfulness practitioner, meditator, and sex therapist David Goldmeier sums it up perfectly in a 2013 article, when he comments on Canadian sex therapist and researcher Rosemary Basson's original theorization of responsive desire via her "circular sexual response cycle": "Basson's (2000) notion of 'responsive desire' rests upon the woman being emotionally willing to agree to intercourse, even though she is not desirous or aroused when she initiates physical interaction. In fact, sexual arousal, for instance breast stimulation at foreplay, can feel quite aversive until she responds. Mindfulness can be very useful in that she can learn to sit with these early aversive physical and emotional feelings until arousal and responsive desire take off."

If mindfulness is ultimately about using meditation, awareness, and, in some cases, "loving-kindness" to be present and non-judgmentally observe yourself and the world around you, in order to reconnect the disconnected mind and body, then it only makes sense that women would be the prime targets for mindful work—including the work of mindful sex. After all, it is women who have historically been framed as categorically disconnected, dissociated, and discordant even as (or perhaps because?) they are so good at multitasking.

The feminization of mindfulness is evident in many domains; mindful parenting and mindful eating are also aimed at women given their more prominent roles in day-to-day household labor or reproductive work and caretaking, and as they are targets of the body enhancement and dieting industries. But it is particularly evident in the realm of mindful sex and desire enhancement. Often, this rehabilitation hinges upon a woman accessing her innate but hidden "sexual vigor" or "sexual arousability" to restructure her own identity so that she can see herself as an "especially sexual woman"[21]—in order to "unlock her sexual drive"—by using mindfulness to "pay attention, to tune into the 'truth' of present-moment bodily sensations and feelings."[22] But again, it also relies on the idea that women are naturally disjointed, that their minds and bodies *need* realignment—and this disconnect is perceived as especially problematic when it hinders "successful" sex.

Sex, then, is not only about servicing a tacitly cis-het male partner, but it is about pursuing your own best life, about being your best self. It is about (self-) pleasure, and (self-)care. But pleasure here, the care

21   Bergner (2009).

22   Brotto (2018), pp. 2, 8.

of the self, is ultimately (and oddly!) a managerial, optimization-oriented, and self-disciplinary practice. And paradoxically, it is a means to an end—the *end* here manifesting in a couple of different ways. We might imagine this end to be "successful" penile-vaginal intercourse, the securing of relationship harmony, or even the reproduction of a happy, healthy, stable, and prosperous society. Damn, ladies! A lot is riding on your desire . . . better get to meditating! And: quick.

Negate Your Desire/Enhance Your Desire: Buddhism, Meditation, and "Awesome" Sex

These paradoxes surrounding mindful sex also contradict the Buddhist teachings from which "mindfulness" originated: teachings which emphasized asceticism, inward focus, and the *negation* of sexual desire.

In a 2017 essay, historian of Buddhism Jeff Wilson describes meditation in the Theravadic Buddhist tradition as the origin of contemporary mindfulness practice. This practice is an instantiation of *vipassana* insight meditation, specifically, which is intended to promote awareness in all aspects of life. In its most common monastic use, however, it was "directed toward developing detachment and equanimity, leading to reduction of sensual desires and the eventual achievement of

dispassion and *nirvana*."[23] This is the central paradox—
that a practice associated with coming to terms with the
mundaneness of life, the inherent state of constant suffering, and even the putrescence of the flesh, and instead
moving toward the *abnegation* of enjoyment and pleasure, is now used to promote "awesome" sex, and has
gone from being used to help patients with serious dysfunction, illness, and impairment (such as from gyneco-
logical cancers) to being tied to the idea that "ordinary
sex can be made even better." The mindful sex industry
is embedded within colonialism and it traffics in cultural
appropriation; here, Eastern meditational practices are
interpreted through the lens of Western cultural values
and belief systems within a neoliberal framework.

Wilson also points to how mindful sex is unquestionably put forward as a "woman's practice":

> One of the most striking aspects of the mindful sex
> movement is its intensely gendered nature . . . men's
> sexual problems are treated with little blue pills,
> while the so-called pink Viagra has turned out to be
> Buddhist meditation practice . . . the science seems
> to reflect social attitudes that suggest men naturally
> want and enjoy frequent sex but as they age their
> biology occasionally fails them (for which a chemical

23   Wilson (2017), p. 155.

> treatment can be procured), while women at every
> life stage are conflicted about whether to even have
> sex and often do not enjoy it. The men's problems
> seem to be in their bodies, whereas the women's
> problems, we are told, lie in their minds . . . [24]

Even though he does not address the aforementioned gendered contemporary sexual response cycles, including the ones which mark women as categorically more "responsive" or "receptive" and sometimes as mind/body "discordant," Wilson makes clear how the entire mindful-sex framework is targeted to cis women, and what its underpinnings are. We see how the realm of experimental studies and clinical research and sex therapy (formerly under the purview of orthodox medicine), and the realm of online and media-oriented popular self-help (previously under the purview of non-clinicians, journalists, and pop-psych bestseller authors), are increasingly merged today, to the point where they are often now indistinguishable.

Self-diagnosis and self-management via the internet only exacerbate this problem—it's now quite difficult to know where one's medical information (or alternative health and wellness advice) is actually coming from. But wherever the information and advice come from, there

24   Wilson (2017), p. 165.

is no question that the takeaway is: You control your own sexual destiny. Desire can be yours. And you should definitely want—and *seek*—to enhance your desire and have "awesome sex," as doing so is good for your health, happiness, and productivity (not to mention the health of your partner, your relationship, your children, and society writ large).

Given this rational, goal-oriented mentality toward health and desire improvement, even as it appears in the form of alternative health movements, it is unsurprising that mindfulness and sex therapy, along with CBT, have now been brought together.

In their seminal book *Human Sexual Response*, published in 1966, second-wave sexology pioneers Masters and Johnson described their method of "sensate focus" as a way of being present with another person's body, without over-attending to either that person's pleasure or one's own pleasure. The technique was meant to disentangle an anxious emotional response from the sexual act itself, so that sexually troubled individuals could overcome their fears and thus their sexual dysfunctions. Many contemporary practitioners say that Masters and Johnson were the first to apply mindfulness in sex therapy via their "sensate focus" techniques. Before it was even cool to do it, then, these mid-twentieth-century behaviorists were bringing mindfulness and meditation into the experimental and therapeutic medical clinic. And this is just more evidence of the long legacy of collapsing CAM and traditional medicine—with clear goals in mind, to be executed by patients willing to try "new" (read: co-opted/westernized) techniques.

Today, sex therapy is increasingly targeted to individuals. Couples rarely go to a sex therapist to work on their issues together; they seek out diagnoses for themselves, individually. Complementary and alternative medicine is becoming more and more popular, widely available, and integrated with orthodox medicine. The world of regular medicine and the world of CAM are increasingly difficult to parse apart—they bleed into each other, and, today, it's often hard to tell the difference. And self-help and self-enhancement techniques—including in the realms of sex and desire—continue to be targeted differently to men and to women, with specific versions designed to enhance "receptive [female] desire" targeted to elite, cis-het, white women (who come to stand in—in this discourse—for "all women").

With all of this in mind, it makes total sense that women are also now the arbiters of mindful sexual practices, and, perhaps most importantly under regimes of neoliberal optimization, that they are expected to work on sex mindfully in the name of their own *pleasure*—in the name of *self-care*. "Always be optimizing," as Tolentino says, now means that you, white ladies, can and should optimize your body, desire, and sex life, too.

And let's not forget that mindfulness is now considered to be an important part of female empowerment—"girl power"—in the twenty-first century. Commodified complementary and alternative medicine is taken up under the sign of what even today's capitalist health and wellness trend trackers are calling the new "fourth wave" of feminism. This is a strange contradiction indeed, which further hinges upon not only a reductively cis and straight vision of femininity and feminine sexuality, but, as we will elaborate in the next chapter, also one that is bourgeois, white, and geographically specific to the Global North.

What can we make of the contradictions inherent in all of this mindful sex talk, and how do we make sense of the strange journey from ascetic Buddhist meditational practices to mindfully enhancing our "receptive" sexual desire in the name of feminist self-care? Where else do we see these contradictions in the world of complementary and alternative health? And, most urgently, are there other—less exploitative, more decolonial—options?

Decolonizing Mindfulness, Meditation, and Yoga: How Do We Do It? Is It Even Possible?

After this deep dive into the commodification of mindfulness as a method of cultivating and optimizing (white) femininity, we want to end this chapter by going back to some of the questions and themes we brought up earlier.

Previously, we mentioned that famed Black Panther Party leaders Ericka Huggins and Angela Davis did yoga, meditated, and practiced mindfulness while imprisoned for their revolutionary political organizing. And we raised the questions: Is it possible for mindfulness to be utilized toward collectivist and revolutionary ends, as a real rupture or break from racial capitalism and colonialism? Or is it really just a way to prepare us to work even harder, next time?

We realize people really like mindfulness, and that meditation truly can be helpful for a variety of ailments and issues. And we know we've kind of dragged the commodified elite white version of these practices through the mud (well, they kind of deserved it, to be honest), but we also do know that there are lots of radical folks out there who use these methods to different ends. Meaning: many awesome people, including social justice fighters and BIPOC revolutionaries, have advocated for the use of mindfulness and meditation to aid their work. So: maybe the real problem here is the way these practices are too often used today (see above)—which is most often *not* toward achieving social justice.

In a YouTube video posted by Afropunk in 2018, Angela Davis makes the case for radical self-care as integral to doing the work of collective social justice, of collective liberation, and as part of the sustainability of continuing that work:

> [Practicing radical self-care] means that we're able to bring our entire selves into the movement. It means that we incorporate into our work as activists ways of acknowledging and hopefully also moving beyond trauma. It means a holistic approach . . . it's very dangerous not to recognize that as we struggle we are attempting to presage the world to come. And the world to come should be one in which we acknowledge collectivity and connections and relations and joy. And if we don't start practicing collective self-care now, there's no way to imagine, much less reach, a time of freedom . . .

Davis makes the collective stakes of taking care of ourselves clear. Not for maximum sexual awesomeness, or to make our nuclear family or romantic partner happy, or to be more productive at our jobs. But instead, as part of a long game in which individuals, who make up a larger collective, maintain themselves and their own energy and their own deep happiness and well-being. Her words emphasize the knowledge that our own health and well-being is always bound up with other people's health and well-being, and that it is possible to take care of ourselves while also caring for each other—that, in fact, they are part of the same project.

This is a very different kind of self-care than what we have been examining so far.

And to be clear: Davis does talk explicitly about doing yoga and meditating while in prison, and she mentions that Huggins taught the other Panthers these tactics, as well. So there must be ways to use mindfulness and meditation and yoga toward revolutionary ends, right? And maybe it's okay to use them in these ways even as they might conflict with some of the original Buddhist and Hindu teachings about them? We don't have the answers to all of these questions, but we are willing to follow the lead of revolutionary BIPOC healers in thinking through these thorny issues.

According to many radical healers, teachers, social workers, and body workers today, there is most definitely a social justice potential to be found in mindfulness, meditation, yoga, and other centering, grounding, and awareness-building practices. This might take a couple of different forms, depending on who you are (i.e., your location within various social and political hierarchies of power).

For instance, according to radical educator and yoga teacher Beth Berila, incorporating mindfulness and meditation into "contemplative pedagogy" in a social justice-centered classroom can be an important part of unlearning oppression (including internalized oppression). It can be a way for students to cultivate introspection, emotional attunement, and compassion, and begin to examine and challenge deeply entrenched narratives they use to interpret the world and their own conditioned responses. Through this "embodied reflexivity," Berila argues that privileged young people can reflect on their own roles in upholding structural oppression, and begin to imagine alternatives, while individuals with less privilege might become more equipped to reflect on how they are affected by these systems. And, of course, we all sit at the nexus of various interlocking social positions, and thus may experience more or less privilege in different times and spaces (and also over the course of our lives).

So: it seems like developing this "contemplative pedagogy" and "embodied reflexivity" could be helpful for everyone—lots of people (not just students) could potentially use mindfulness to sit with their own defensiveness (about their own roles in supporting racism, sexism, classism, and colonialism), and use that to move forward with a different orientation. Even though using mindfulness feels most often like an individual thing, the focus here is different, as it's not about self-improvement for self-improvement's sake.

Using mindfulness as part of a social justice-focused practice has definitely been dismissed by some organizers and activists as just another way to protect privileged people from facing their own racism, classism, sexism, homophobia, transphobia, and ableism. It is also seen by some as not aiding—or even as *impeding*—a serious focus on doing the hard and real work of dismantling systems of oppression and systemic violence. Another critique is that mindfulness can actually mask trauma, or push marginalized folks to discount or ignore their own traumatic experiences in the name of "being present" or "in the moment." We take these critiques seriously, and recognize that radical BIPOC organizers have different attitudes toward utilizing these practices.

Some social justice activists, including those who put together some thoughtful self-care resources for www.therapychanges.com, suggest that practicing mindfulness and meditation could actually be a way for marginalized folks to take a much-needed break from always being put in the position of being "experts"—on racism, colonialism, oppression, etc. But: the fact that the women leaders of the BPP were the ones teaching mindfulness and meditation to the men in the group simultaneously points to the fact that not only were they the ones who really needed a serious break from being "racism(/sexism) experts," but also that the work of teaching self-care practices to movement-builders can end up being one more form of feminized labor.

So we will keep pondering: what is it about self-care that makes women more likely to learn and practice it? To *need* it? But then also to be put in a position where they are expected to teach it and its value to others (read: men) in the movement? Self-care, then, even in this more radical context, can still sometimes (paradoxically) be a form of women's reproductive labor . . .

It seems to us that using mindfulness and meditation among similar methods toward anti-oppressive ends is at least worth exploring, in any case, and it may be possible to do this type of self-care *right*—that is, when oppressed people are in charge of the process (but: simultaneously not unduly burdened—and this is definitely a fine line that must be considered and a difficult balance).

In a 2015 essay for the blog Decolonizing Yoga, Susanna Barkataki, desi yoga teacher and practitioner, also advocates for using mindfulness, meditation, and yoga toward decolonial ends—while thoroughly critiquing the "yoga-industrial-complex." Barkataki argues that due to westernization and commodification by elite white people, yoga is going through a "second colonization" (the first colonization was when yoga and Ayurveda were banned in India, under British rule). She says that yoga cannot be solely about physical mastery or "stress reduction," and emphasizes the aspects of yoga that were meant to increase *awareness*—"yoga means liberation from every construct, including that of race, gender, time, space, location, identity, and even history herself." She mentions a few ways that practitioners can stop re-colonizing yoga, including through exploring, learning, and citing correct cultural references when teaching and practicing yoga, and asking one's self the "hard" questions, like: "For whom is yoga accessible today and how might that be a legacy of past injustices that we have the opportunity to address through our teaching practice and our lives?"

Some activists have also put forward the idea of "*neuro*decolonization" as a mode of undoing the psychic effects of coloniality on the brain and patterns of thinking.[25] For his website www.indigenousmindful-ness.com, sociologist, social worker, and citizen of the Three Affiliated Tribes (Mandan, Hidatsa, and Arikara),

25   This coinage invokes the work of Ngũgĩ wa Thiong'o, particularly his *Decolonising the Mind: The Politics of Language in African Literature*, originally published in 1986, in addition to the revolutionary anti-colonial theory of Frantz Fanon.

Michael Yellow Bird, says that mindfulness practices are common to Indigenous cultures, but have been stripped away from Indigenous practitioners in the wake of colonialism and neo-colonialism (including as white settlers have co-opted and commodified these practices). He argues for taking back these practices, and seeks to re-integrate them into Indigenous communities, as a way for Indigenous people—who disproportionately experience so many health issues from diabetes to substance use disorders to depression and post-traumatic stress disorder—to rewire their neural networks and thus find relief and well-being. And he explicitly frames these ill health issues as the effects of racism, colonialism, and transgenerational trauma, to which so many BIPOC individuals have been subjected.

We will return to radical and decolonial possibilities for self-care, including in the form of mindfulness, meditation, and yoga practices, at the end of this book. But first, we have to walk you through a couple more examples of the *self-care industrial complex* and show you how and why it has gotten these practices so desperately wrong—and in the process, actually caused harm to marginalized populations, while elite white settlers (including lady venture capitalists!) reap the benefits.

Chapter 2

MARKETING SELF-CARE: FROM FEMTECH AND BIOHACKING TO PAINMOONS AND EXTREME TRAVEL

Have you ever googled "self-care"? Well, you may be unsurprised to hear that we have. And during our internet research expeditions, we have found a *ton* of tropes and truisms, such as from the popular VeryWell Mind website, which defines self-care as "a conscious act that one takes in order to promote their own physical, mental, and emotional health."[26] In this particular mental health promotion website's discussion of "stress reduction," the merits of "self-care" are emphasized, alongside "spirituality" (devoid of any cultural or religious context) and "mindful living" (we are not exactly sure what this means). Examples of self-care in such venues tend to include things like taking a bath, meditating or practicing mindfulness, sleeping late, "taking time" for one's self, doing yoga, or getting a massage—and these acts of self-support are almost always individualized and feminized (that is, racially non-specific women are posited as needing self-care the most, sometimes due to their evolutionary [!] proclivity for too much multi-tasking, as we discussed in the last chapter).

26   Scott (2022).

On other platforms, such as the Active Minds web-site, tips for taking time for one's self are interspersed alongside mantras like "we all experience times where we need to take a step back and focus on ourselves," "self-care is not selfish," and "you must fill your own cup before you can pour into others."[27] These at-times vague and vapid mantras are often also accompanied by images of women "taking care" of themselves. For example, as I write this, I am looking at a photo next to a blurb about self-care that features what appears to be a white cis woman's hand holding a book, next to a laptop that has been closed and put down, and a cup of tea. A cat joins her in her pursuit of leisure. The cat is very cute.

Feminine self-care is linked, then, to refueling one's self so that one may be of better service to others. But the implicit "others" who will be more efficiently cared for in way too many of these popular discussions of women's self-care, today as in the past, consist of a lady's immediate nuclear family members, such as her husband and children. *These* are the people she should really be striving to care for better, apparently . . . a far cry from Angela Davis and Ericka Huggins meditating and doing

---

27   https://www.activeminds.org/about-mental-health/self-care/.

yoga in order to prepare themselves to fight for racial justice (and/or to give themselves a grounding and centering break from the role thrust upon them as "experts" on racism and sexism).

In broad strokes, women's health is further linked to the health of "society." This way of thinking about the importance of self-care for women—as always in the service of others—is not only evident on media outlets. At industry-wide conferences such as the "Illuminations" Women's Health Conference in Vancouver, British Columbia, held in January 2020, the importance of women's health—as the key to broader societal improvement, and as a way to support the enhancement of children's health and men's health— was a prominent theme. Apparently, one of the main reasons women should strive to be healthy is because that will help everyone else (i.e., men and children) be healthier, too. This is suggested via a series of tweets memorializing the conference, including this one on January 23 from the B.C. Women's Health Foundation: "The outcomes of when we focus on research in women's health: they benefit, their children benefit and men benefit. We focus on women's health because everyone benefits . . ." Regarding a health report published by the

Foundation earlier that fall, another tweeter tweeted: "When women thrive, all of society benefits . . ."[28]

Within this same logic, Michelle Murphy (the feminist historian of science we mentioned in the Introduction) describes the "Girl Effect" and "Invest in a Girl" campaigns, in which the health of young women is used as a benchmark for economic prosperity. In her 2017 book, *The Economization of Life,* Murphy describes how foreign policy, international development schemes, and so-called humanitarian efforts by countries in the Global North use "women's health" (generally based on data from the Global South) as an indicator of the broader social health and future development potential of communities, nations, and the world.[29]

And global commerce organizations like the International Monetary Fund and the World Bank publish reports about how "investing" in women's health and well-being is *strategic*; again, primarily because it's beneficial for the world economy. In a 2017 blog post for

28   See https://twitter.com/BCWomensFdn/status/ 1220462808267132929 and https://twitter.com/ SexualHealthRN/status/1181985013975240704.

29   For more on this, see info on "The Girl Effect" https://www. girleffect.org/ and the "Invest in a Girl" campaign https:// womendeliver.org/wp-content/uploads/2017/03/Deliver-for -Good-Booklet.pdf.

the World Bank, Patricio Marquez writes: "We know that healthy women are at the core of healthy societies. The health of women is not, however, innate to any society. Development experience has shown that deliberate policies and programmatic strategies aimed at nurturing women's health and well-being across the life cycle are vital for realizing the full potential of women and girls."

This all sounds great, right? Women's needs are being attended to; who cares how it happens? The problem is that there are some insidious mandates snuck in here in this rhetoric of "realizing *the full potential* of women and girls"—not only are women in the Global South expected to be healthy, and educated, and good prosperous citizens (in accordance with western, white, bourgeois standards for all of these things), but their well-being is really only considered insofar as it is part of an investment strategy. Improving women's health and education and opportunities then is not really about making life better for *actual women and girls* but rather is a way of improving the economic health of the nations and regions these women and girls come to represent, and about harvesting their potential for the "health" of the world market. "Women and girls," then, really just add up to feminized populations to be managed, speculated upon, and invested in; they're not actual people to be concerned about. And "women's well-being" becomes synonymous with enhanced gross domestic product (GDP)—and a variety of other economic indicators.

It is easy to see how *self-care*, in its contemporary, western, feminized form, as a corollary, is about being more efficient, effective, and better at caring for others, but not necessarily about directly caring for underserved populations or broader communities (this would be more in keeping with the spirit of self-care as it was originally described in revolutionary anti-capitalist, anti-racist, queer, feminist, and disability justice spaces). Instead, we have women in the Global South symbolizing improvements in the world economy and international relations, while women in the Global North are rolling out business ventures to better pamper themselves (and their nuclear families).

And: we now have more than one version of self-care for women wherein the benefits are actually directed toward others—one is when a woman can better care for her immediate (tacitly wealthy, white, cis-het, nuclear) family members, and the other is when "women's health" in the abstract is correlated with the health of populations, nation-states, and/or markets.

In an interesting (and somewhat perverse) twist, however, the most popular contemporary version of elite feminine self-care in the Global North today actually folds these aspects together, bringing it all back around, and in the process, ultimately re-centers the self: caring for others is good because it's good for *you.*

As we will explain, this twisted iteration encapsulates the newest phase of self-care today. The seemingly inverted and distorted idea is that "community care" is *good for the self*—doing social justice work (broadly construed) which emphasizes diversity, equity, inclusion, and even "intersectionality," is *personally* beneficial, and that's really the reason to do it. Important to note is that all of these versions of feminized self-care are fully compatible with neoliberalism and the commodification of care, and they are all rooted in white liberal feminism.

Ancient, Sacred, Sensual: Femininity Itself as a Form of Care

Women's self-care today is a highly lucrative market. Some websites and pop culture venues make the white feminization and commodification of self-care more explicit than others. And monetized self-care is often, in another contortion, linked to descriptions of "ancient" or "sacred" femininity—bringing us right back to the discussions of co-optation, appropriation, and neoliberal optimization with which we began this book.

Let's start with this example: the website for The Feminine, described as "an online platform dedicated to empowering women all over the world to trust their voice, follow their heart and embrace their womanhood—with no fear and no shame," CEO, platform founder, podcast host, and transformational coach Oana Stoianovici encourages women to embrace their "sacred femininity" and enhance their own sensuality as a mode of self-care. In a post on www.thefeminine.com, a blogger and friend of the founder writes:

> In ancient times, women used the creation of the sacred space as a way to feel guarded and protected. Not by a man, but by their own beating hearts. This gave them access to start the mature work of discovering the gifts of The Feminine. It gave them courage to be vulnerable and walk with their own shadows, hidden gifts, and untamed voices, long enough until they grew strong and fierce and were ready to own who they are and meet the outside world expecting nothing in return and being ready to offer everything . . . the sacred space allows you to become soft and gentle and patient with yourself. It allows your Heart to awaken and it gives you access to letting go of any conditioning, so that you can surrender to your true rhythm and to your true voice.

Although it is not entirely clear to us what a "sacred space" is, we must admit that upon perusing this website, we felt excited by the prospect of being immersed in such a space, and couldn't help ourselves from downloading the podcast episode on "listening to one's 'inner child.'"

The Feminine—and associated podcast *The Feminine #Uncut*—is just one prototypical example that brings these themes together in an especially obvious way. We did listen to some of the podcasts, including one episode entitled "The Essential Guide to Meditation (The Feminine Way)." In this episode, host Oana seeks to understand how and why men and women meditate differently (who knew?!), and how women can embrace and enhance their particular feminine version of meditation. Apparently, women need to "submit" more than men do when meditating, specifically to their own feminine energy, which is less "structured" than masculine energy, and more about flow, tuning into the earth's natural rhythms and the rhythms of their own female bodies, holding hands, crying, laughing, and dancing naked in the moonlight and maybe howling at the moon, all in order to sacredly embrace one's feminine heart and, most importantly, womb? (Yes, she says all of these things pretty much verbatim.) Honestly, this one was kind of boring and a little hard to follow, so we stopped listening about halfway through . . .

Many other outlets suggest similar connections among femininity, spirituality, and the sacred—and, more and more often, *empowerment*—and put forward suggestions for enhancing and optimizing these and the connections among them. Other popular podcasts that focus even more on the "empowerment" piece (and which also imbue women's self-care and self-improvement with the power to save the world) include: *The Feminine CEO* (in which host Jessica Riverson shares tips on how to "embody a NEW feminine model of success balancing soul and strategy . . . in a place where Inner Priestess meets CEO"), *Feminine Power Time* (in which host Christine Arylo helps the listener tap into "Divine Feminine Wisdom" in a place where "mystic and MBA meet"), and *Feminine & Fulfilled* (in which the listener is encouraged to "join the conversation to rise [sic] the feminine power that will bring our world back to balance again"). These are just a few of the many, many podcasts that push feminized and empowering self-help—and there are many that connect to sexual well-being as a core aspect of health and optimization, as well.[30]

As a reminder from the previous chapter: self-care, as it pertains to the figure of the white, middle-class

---

30 Another notable example in this vein is Mama Gena and her School of Womanly Arts. Mama Gena is an NYC-based motivational speaker with a training program and inspirational experience protocol whose message is consistent: "embrace your feminine side, because it gives you the power to succeed in relationships, in work, and in life." Entry into the Mama Gena society is steep: Her three-weekend "Mastery" course costs $5,950, and the nine-month "Creation" course is $12,000. See Rowland (2020) for an in-depth discussion of Mama Gena's program.

housewife, is connected to taking time off from the broader practices of housework and carework—with the goal of doing that work better. But what can we make of the connection between self-care and feminized labor if the hypothetical woman being marketed to today (or, in many cases, *doing* the marketing) is a career girl instead of a housewife? When her domestic responsibilities have (once again) been outsourced to poor women, immigrant women, and women from the Global South—to make time and space for her to "get ahead"? When they have been outsourced to flashy products and automated via a variety of new technologies?

In today's market, the idea is that self-care is a form of *self-optimization*—it is less and less about caring for others (even cis-het, white, bourgeois, nuclear family-related others) or reproducing the life of the home and the family. Instead, contemporary self-care involves reproducing one's own *feminine* self—as a lifestyle, as a persona, and as a brand.

Marketing Feminine Care (and We Don't [Only] Mean Tampons and Maxi Pads): New Form, New Content, New Bottom Line

The market and research industry for white feminine self-care today runs the gamut in terms of legitimacy. There are plenty of credentialed, well-respected doctors and scientists who study the benefits of self-care (e.g., via mindful sex) as an important aspect of women's health, on the one side. Then there's Gwyneth Paltrow and Goop, on the other.

Importantly, however, the self-care, mindfulness, and wellness industry *in its entirety* and *taken as a whole* articulates and traffics in a certain femininity: white, bourgeois, cisgender, and heteronormative.

And now that science, spirituality, and self-help seem to ever more frequently bleed into each other, to the point that they are often indistinguishable, we wonder how much really separates the two ("legitimate" vs. "snake oil") poles of the self-care/wellness spectrum.

One thing that *could* be said to separate the credentialed medical practitioners from the ancient femininity snake-oil marketeers is, well, the bottom line. And today, the bottom line for the wellness industry or self-care market is truly immense and only getting bigger. As we noted in the Introduction, the global wellness economy was valued at $4.9 trillion in 2019 and is projected to reach nearly $7.0 trillion by 2025.

Within this market, a white feminization can be observed in terms of both the *content* (what is sold) as well as the *form* of capitalist exchange (how it is sold).

Avenues like "FemTech," which includes apps for things like fertility solutions, period tracking, pregnancy

and nursing care, women's sexual wellness, and "reproductive system" health care—are all made available and
consumable via e-commerce modalities (so mainly the
shift is in content, but also a little in form). The 2018
Global Wellness Summit report sums it up: "One of the
most exciting wellness trends, period (and yes, 'solving' for women's periods is part of it) is the explosion of
women doctors, technologists, scientists, designers and
entrepreneurs unleashing a waterfall of smart 'I get it'
products and technology solutions aimed at cracking the
code for women's unique needs, bodies and sexuality."
And while we unquestionably support people being able
to use technology to do things like track menstruation
and other such bodily experiences (particularly in a
post-*Roe* US), we are not sure why the apps themselves
need to be drenched in the color pink or what the feminine "code" is that needs to be "cracked" here.

"Biohacking"—a DIY form of health care implemented to enhance and get "in tune" with one's own
biology, also used to sell new alternative health products—is another specifically gendered wellness or
self-care technology. [31] Biohacking has traditionally

31   From https://www.parsleyhealth.com/blog/biohacking
     -women-101/: "Biohacking is just about using the latest science
     and practical guidance to improve how you feel every day…

been more often associated with men—specifically men who made their fortunes in the tech sector before turning their skillset to hacking the body and mind in order to optimize their own health and fitness.

One recent example of how biohacking is masculinized and targeted to men is the new trend "dopamine fasting": the idea is that a busy and successful man, most often employed in tech (say, in Silicon Valley), will intentionally avoid anything that might make him feel happy and good, from sex to saying hello to sandwiches, for a specified period of time, so that once he re-engages with the world he will be flooded with dopamine and feel *great*. So this form of biohacking is targeted to men, in the vein of mindful, embodied asceticism. The tagline for a 2019 article in *The New York Times* by Nellie Bowles on the topic—"how to feel nothing now, in order to feel more later"—says it all.

A blogger for Parsley Health, one of the pioneer, preeminent, and most successful New York City-based (although they're all over the country now) functional medicine groups, argues that women can be just as good

according to Dave Asprey, 'biohacking is the art and science of changing the environment around you and inside you, so you have more control over your own biology.' It allows us to optimize the body's potential and become the 'absolute best version of ourselves.'"

at biohacking as men are—they just need to do it a bit differently:

> It could be argued that women are the original bio-hackers. We have been manipulating our hormones to control pregnancy starting thousands of years ago using lunaception (tracking [menstrual] cycles to the moon) and more modern ways via birth control pills. Generally, women are more in tune with their bodies which makes us prime candidates for biohacking. So what's the difference between biohacking for men vs. women? It's all about those hormones.

The idea behind "contextual commerce" further sums up trends in the new feminized neoliberal capitalist form and content (and their collapse). According to *TechCrunch*, contextual commerce is the potentially "'game-changing' idea that merchants can seamlessly implement purchase opportunities into everyday activities and natural environments. In other words, people can buy anything, anytime, anywhere, with the click of a button . . . or even just their voice. It's the concept behind the buy buttons you've seen rolling out on platforms like Instagram, Pinterest, and Facebook."

"BFF marketing" takes this concept even further, and fully encapsulates the elite, white, cis-heteronormative femininity of these new markets: "Chatty, inclusive and intimate, this approach—predicated on the notion that a brand is your 'best friend forever,' thinks you're special, and is designing products especially for *you*—is the core narrative behind the rise of some of the most successful direct-to-consumer womenswear and beauty brands in the marketplace right now," says journalist Pandora Sykes.

Sykes, writing for *Business of Fashion*, interviews various women execs about their thoughts on the direction of fem-marketing, including Maggie Winter, chief executive and co-founder of the sustainable, season-less brand AYR ("All Year Round"), who states: "The customer calls the shots. She's in charge." AYR is 80 percent direct-to-consumer and uses "gal-pal-style" e-mail newsletters to drive e-commerce sales. "'Your social media feed. Designed to make you feel good sometimes, bad other times. Unlike these jeans which are designed to make you feel amazing 24/7,' reads one newsletter from Summer 2017"—and Sykes states that the strategy appears to be working, as site traffic driven by e-mails is up 60 percent in the last year (since 2017). "Just because the goal is to drive revenue, doesn't mean that dialogue has to be impersonal and aggressive," CEO Winter is quoted as stating in the interview for *BoF*. The connection to female empowerment and "fourth wave feminism" is clarified further:

"The shtick is: 'We gotchu girl,'" says Lucie Green, chief global futurist at marketing communications agency, J. Walter Thompson. [She goes on:] "This inclusive, Lena Dunham-type dialogue taps into fourth wave feminism, where the direct-to-consumer brands are often symbiotically linked to having a female founder. The story of the brand becomes a case of female empowerment and you're encouraged to support them not just as a consumer, but as a supporter of their story." At Goop, Gwyneth Paltrow has "baked herself into the product," while Reese Witherspoon places herself squarely at the centre of her brand, Draper James, inhabiting the role of the ultimate Southern belle.

So: the brand must be "cute" and *also* "empowering"— offering women something they haven't felt like they've had full control over, something that's been missing, but on "their terms." Hence, the birth of the lifestyle brand and its obvious distribution modality—BFF marketing.

Goop, of course, is the quintessential lifestyle brand and one of the most well-known and successfully monetized pioneers in this realm—effortlessly combining new (feminized) content with new (feminized) forms of capitalist exchange. We couldn't possibly write a book about decolonizing self-care without investigating Goop.

The now multi-million-dollar company began as a newsletter compiled by Gwyneth Paltrow (the titular

"GP" for which "Goop" is named—hence Paltrow's nickname, used by many of her fans) in 2008. Initially, the letter was meant to offer recipes, health and beauty advice, lists of the "best" places to go and things to do while, for instance, on holiday in a given locale, and to connect GP's fans—to each other, to her, but most importantly, to her way of life. To the things she loves. To the coolest stuff around. According to Taffy Brodesser-Akner, writing for *The New York Times* in 2018, "Goop's ethic was this: that having beautiful things sometimes costs money; finding beautiful things was sometimes a result of an immense privilege; but a lack of that privilege didn't mean you shouldn't have those things. Besides, just because some people cannot afford it doesn't mean that no one can and that no one should want it. If this bothered anyone, well, the newsletter content was free, and so were the recipes for turkey ragù and banana-nut muffins." GP is the perfect example (and she really does seem perfect, doesn't she? A little too perfect, ugh . . .) of an elite white woman in the Global North who *was* able to access the venture capital that the vast majority of women around the world—as we described in the Introduction to this book—do not have access to.

The cheapest ticket to GP's retreats are $500 and the VIP is sometimes up to $4,500 (or so we've heard). In another recent *Times* article, Alexandra Jacobs reports that, "At Goop retreats you can buy probiotic drinks flavored with peach and passion fruit, made by Tropicana, which is owned by Pepsi—showing just how thoroughly the philosophy of 'gut health,' championed to some derision by Ms. Paltrow and several in her medical retinue, has infiltrated the corporate mainstream." Jacobs describes attending a Goop retreat, which used the tagline "In Goop Health," where she learned about the different tiers of payment and access, in addition to the broader philosophy of Goop. There was a spectrum of payment options—from the "lapis" members (the plebeians, whose entry was $500) to the "clear quartz" (the first-class payers; at this retreat, the highest level was a mere $1,500).

Everyone also had varying levels of access to everything from facial-toning massages to meditative sound baths to shamanic crystal readings to vitamin-fortified intravenous drips to interactions with GP herself during cocktail hours and garden luncheons. Jacobs quotes Paltrow: "I like the idea that wellness for us is a broader thing—it's not just 'oh go eat some quinoa in a corner and meditate' . . . it's like 'no, we're modern women and we want to feel good and optimize our lives in a lot of different ways.'" Optimized, indeed.

Since its inception, Goop has attracted more than $82 million in outside funding, and was projected to generate between $90 million and $120 million in revenue in 2018. Goop focuses on feminine inspiration, women's empowerment, sexual enhancement, health, beauty, travel, everything associated with The Good Life. But, perhaps more specifically, Goop deals in *aspiration*. While the blog content on the website is free, Paltrow has repeatedly defended the high price point of her products and tickets to her summits, stating that "our stuff is beautiful; you can't make these things mass-market."

If you can't afford Goop products, in other words, you should certainly aspire to.

Selling Sexiness: The Gender Binary, Sexual Difference, and Receptive Femininity as Commodity Redux (Again, and Again . . . and Again)

The health benefits of specifically woman-targeted technologies and products are a key focus in wellness markets, in general, and in Goop's marketplace in particular. Goop's promotion of "yoni eggs" (made of jade and rose quartz) and "vaginal steaming" (for gynecological/reproductive health and sexual empowerment?) are just two examples here—and they have been roundly critiqued by medical professionals as hack science and snake oil products.[32] These vagina-enhancing devices and concepts are only one piece of a broader Goop catalogue that makes white, bourgeois, cis-het femininity a commodity, a project, and a lifestyle to be achieved—you can also buy a gorgeous soft sweater, learn about "grieving the loss of a life you wanted," and discover the health benefits of Tantric sex.

And so we hear the same story: sex is the key to "becoming your best self" in Goop and similar non-/quasi-medical self-help venues, just as it is in the medical sphere. For instance, in a Goop interview on Tantra with Michaela Boehm, internationally renowned expert on intimacy, relationships, and sexuality, the dialogue somehow veers into a discussion of masculinity, femininity, and the purportedly boring nature of equality. According to Boehm:

---

32 Some of the very proponents of mindful sexuality, feminine self-care, and women's health in the more reputable and legitimate medical/scientific realm are, in fact, staunch critics of the Goopier version. Dr. Jen Gunter (2019a,b) is perhaps the most vocal critic of Goopy commodification and "snake oil"—as she argues that Goop perpetuates false ideas about women's health and profits off of women's insecurities, including via expensive and potentially dangerous products like the jade yoni egg.

> For many women, the idea of coming home from
> work and being greeted at the door by a smiling,
> apron-clad husband actually feels disconcerting—
> even though the idea of a husband who makes din-
> ner is very appealing. However, with a subtle shift—
> coming home to a husband who directs you to have
> a glass of wine while he finishes up dinner prep
> suddenly sounds quite sexy . . . the direction—the
> assumption of the masculine aspect—is a subtle but
> essential necessity.

There are innumerable examples of extremely profitable companies today that focus on women, that target women's sexuality and desire, and which emphasize the importance of female sexual empowerment. Being sexually empowered and having "good" sex are subtly positioned as feminine responsibilities or duties (toward conviviality, generosity, and hospitality—including to one's self), and mindfulness is the vehicle or modality to achieve these ends, as described in the previous chapter. Sexual well-being, then, is most certainly a through-line from the more medically legitimate sphere to the more popular self-help sphere. And again, the medical, complementary/alternative, and commodified self-help spheres are not so separate anymore . . .

One notorious example that has received a ton of attention over the last decade—and critical scrutiny for its eventually-revealed cult-like and multi-level-marketing or pyramid scheme status—is OneTaste.[33]

Founded by Nicole Daedone in San Francisco in the early 2000s, OneTaste came to define itself as a business dedicated to researching and teaching the practices of slow sex and Orgasmic Meditation or "OM"—a trademarked procedure that typically involves a cisgender man using a gloved, lubricated fingertip to stroke a cisgender woman's clitoris for approximately fifteen minutes. Though it embraces certain tenets based in "Eastern philosophy," OneTaste's central focus has been on female orgasm and sexuality, especially through OM. During the company's rapid ascent (and before its very quick crash), the San Francisco and later Los Angeles and New York City-based company made $12 million in revenue in 2017 and then expanded to Atlanta, Chicago, Minneapolis, and Washington. It also partnered with companies like Odwalla, and according to former CEO Joanna Van Vleck, quoted in an article by Ellen Huet for *Bloomberg Businessweek* in 2018, "OneTaste is the Whole Foods of sexuality—the organic, good-for-you version."

33   After being investigated by the FBI for sex trafficking, "prostitution," and violations of labor law beginning in 2018, OneTaste shut its doors and rebranded itself as "The Institute of OM": https://instituteofom.com/.

OneTaste is perhaps an outlier in the wellness arena, having been the subject of so much public criticism for being a sex cult/Ponzi scheme and now undergoing investigation by the FBI due to trafficking allegations. But the group's notoriety clearly demonstrates how sexual fulfillment—and specifically female pleasure—becomes something to be capitalized upon in pseudo-medical or quasi-medical spaces. This capitalization not only sells products but is also an example of a lifestyle built around calling up, utilizing, and instrumentalizing heterosexual desire and gynocentric, cis-feminine pleasure.

This "always be optimizing" mentality regarding the productive nature of female sexuality is made clear in a TED Talk featuring Daedone, recorded in 2011 well before the sex-cult-and-multi-level-marketing-scandal part of the story made international news. Throughout the talk, Daedone emphasizes the notion that enhancing female pleasure is not only good for women, it's good for men, it's good for families, it's good for the whole world (That's right, folks! You've heard this one before: healthy women = healthy populations/nation-states/markets).

As we have described, this is a refrain echoed by many in the mindful sex and sexual wellness sphere, but it is really hammered home by Daedone in this early talk entitled "Orgasm: The Cure for Hunger in the

Western Woman"—which, at the time of this writing, has been viewed almost two and a half million times on YouTube. In it, Daedone describes how female orgasm is "vital for every single woman on the planet," that "it's not so bad for the guys either," and that it "roots our fundamental capacity for connection." The women who come to OneTaste, they are "clamoring to be sated," and chanting the "Western woman's mantra": "I work too hard, I eat too much, I diet too much, I drink too much, I shop too much, I give too much, and still there is this sense of hunger that I can't touch." Poetic.

This elite whitewashed sexual difference discourse reverberates throughout the talk, and binary gender stereotypes make up the underlying foundation. Daedone describes how she learned the OM technique from a cis man, at a (sex?) party, who stroked the upper left quadrant of her clitoris (seemingly in a kind of meditative, non-sexual way?). Nothing happened at the time, because she was too "in her head." But the whole experience made her cry, and this man made something begin to "thaw" in her, because she had "never been looked at or felt that kind of compassion in that area before."

Again, this is a common refrain across discourses—the modern woman is too stressed out and too busy multi-tasking to be able to connect with her own natural, free-flowing, physiological sexual arousal (she might even be evolutionarily mind-body "discordant"). But: sexual pleasure is her *birthright* and pursuing it is an integral form of self-care. She deserves maximum sexual awesomeness, dammit!

Daedone ends the talk by describing how female pleasure will save the planet: "The Dalai Lama has said that it will be 'Western woman who changes the world.'" She acknowledges that this is a controversial statement because it presumes that Western women are above other women in terms of changing the world. Daedone, however, has a different issue with it—she thinks that it will be "turned on" women around the world, and "those who dare to stroke us" who will "actually change the world, by feeding this desire for connection that we *all* have!"

Here, we have a blueprint for how sexual pleasure will heal women, men, and once again, the earth itself.

Transform the Pain Away: Extreme Travel & the Most Decadent Self-Care

Extreme and "transformational" travel is a hot new wellness and self-care trend, and extends the notion that the pursuit of pleasure and connection is a (white) woman's birthright. An examination of the self-care travel industry reveals an inverse relationship between the pleasure and empowerment of wealthy white women, on the one hand, and the deplorable treatment and labor conditions of other feminized folks around the world, on the other. Elite travel today goes well beyond the typical beach vacation that a woman might take with her "girlfriends" in times past. Now (in spite of an ongoing global pandemic!), the most important thing is to push your own limits, have new and exciting experiences, and ultimately, to recreate yourself, to recreate your very identity.

Take, for example, the Borgo Egnazia Tarant Wellness Retreat in Puglia, Italy. According to the website:

> The program is all about wild catharsis about matters of the heart, whether you've just suffered a breakup or your sex drive is gone. Sessions span everything from dancing to drums, "laughing and screaming in primordial ways," tambourine banging, (simulated) sword fights, "intense sessions" with the resident shaman, and some mind-melting treatments in the underground candlelit spa . . . all aimed at transforming women's feelings of sadness, anger, embarrassment, and self-loathing into a heady new self-empowerment.

The retreat represents the world-class quintessence of transformational wellness travel, and exists alongside the new trends of "painmoons," "divorce/break-up parties," and "mumcations"—where wealthy or middle-class, middle-aged, and most often cisgender, heterosexual, white women can reconnect with and in some cases reinvent themselves through "extreme wellness."

Rythmia Life Advancement Center is another example—at a beautiful, all-inclusive, medically licensed, luxury resort and retreat center in Guanacaste, Costa Rica, travelers can take ayahuasca and other hallucinogens and psychedelic drugs in order to expand their consciousness, sometimes with the help of an authentic shaman from the region (for a higher price point, of course). According to the website, guests will "awaken to your highest potential through the Rythmia Way Program." Ayahuasca ceremonies, yoga, metaphysics classes, hydrocolonic cleanses, transformational breathwork, massage, and farm to table organic food are all included (for as low as $299 per night!). This does sound truly transformational and we have no doubt that a visit would change us forever (and perhaps also usher in world peace?).

On "Super She Island" a wellness retreat has been set up in a wooded, remote, private island in the Baltic sea off the coast of Finland. According to the 2018 Global Wellness Summit Report, "Super She Island" is "only open to women who apply for membership (only ten stay at a time), where they're immersed in yoga, saunas, meditation, farm-to-table cooking, and roam freely across the wild island. Its philosophy is that women need to spend time with other women to be happy and need places where they can recalibrate without distractions."

Yes, this sounds great for these undistracted, nature-immersed ladies, but the grotesque irony of fomenting "women's empowerment" at the expense of occupying and colonizing a literal island is pretty unreal, in our opinion. Also: we can't really wrap our heads around the second-wavey-ness of the Super She Island "feminist" philosophy (women need to spend time with other women without distractions what?). The seamless rebranding of cultural feminism (the idea that "women," as a group, are nice and kind and essentially empathic and harmoniously in tune with nature or something) under the sign of elite, white, (neo)liberal feminism is breathtaking—not to mention utterly jaw-dropping in its complete lack of self-awareness.

The deeply problematic relationship that many of the most decadent trends and companies in the women's self-care industry has with local communities and Indigenous land is further exemplified by the company WHOA Travel (i.e., "Women High on Adventure"). WHOA caters to adventurous women invested in truly extreme and transformational travel experiences and "has taken women on 'kick ass' adventures in sixty-five countries . . . expeditions include a trek to the base camp of Mount Everest and Kilimanjaro trips (one will culminate on International Women's Day . . . yikes!). And WHOA doesn't just focus on the wellness of their travelers, but is expressly committed to creating "meaningful, authentic connections" with the women and children who live at their destinations.

For instance, for their Kilimanjaro treks, guests stay at a non-profit hotel that funds a local school, and traveler fees sponsor two local women to join every climb. Once again, this social justice-esque cherry on top sounds very nice for these elite adventurous women, but we cannot stomach the idea that "giving back" here means inviting two women who already live in a place (a place where these other adventurous women are tourists!) to join a hiking or climbing expedition, in their own home, on their own native land.

Finally, sometimes holistic wellness, extreme and transformational travel, and mindful sex workshops and Tantra trainings are brought together (for those who can afford it).

In the recent Netflix series *(Un)Well*, self-proclaimed teacher, healer, and energy worker Sasha Cobra, in an interview at her retreat center in Tepotzotlán, Mexico, states that she "is Tantra." Cobra had "an informal training with a man that had been doing this work for years," which was the beginning of "the work" for her. "How do you relate to your sexual energy?" she asks. For $250 an hour for an online consultation and $275 for an in-person consult, she will show you (if you want regenerating energy/bodywork, it will be $600 for an online session and up to $2,200 for an in-person, according to her website).

Cobra tell us that orgasmic energy cleanses the body from trauma—it's a purification process. In an online session with several clients on skype (depicted on an episode of *[Un]Well*), she begins the online tantra class: "For the men, bring your awareness to your genitals, for the women, bring your awareness to your heart area . . . make love to your environment." Tantra is allowing life to live through you. You are an orgasm. According to Cobra: "Some people are great at painting, some people are great musicians, some people are great cooks, I just happen to give people full body orgasms."

In her women-only "Opening to Pleasure" workshop, Cobra says: "We're not [only] exploring pleasure, we're actually exploring health, we're exploring what it means to be a woman, and the way that we do that is through pleasure. And pleasure and sensuality is the medicine, especially for the female body . . . women are always waiting for the right man—the right man for what?! This is a workshop about *empowering women . . .* " She emphasizes the importance of moaning, groaning, screaming, and growling during the session, and at one moment points to her throat and says: "Keep *this* vagina open." (Wut?) At the end of the interview, she states: "Women are orgasmicness, women are sex. And they've been told to be good girls their whole life. So they shut themselves down, they pretend, and they hurt themselves with that. When you give women permission to express their sensuality, it's extremely empowering."

This last part especially really does sounds great, and we agree that women (and people of all genders!) should have autonomy and control over their bodies and sexualities. Seriously. The emphasis on connection, sharing of energy, and healing of trauma is powerful indeed, and it's unsurprising that so many folks, who lead such disconnected and isolated lives, desire to revive themselves to this end. But the ways in which this revival becomes tethered to western binary sexual difference, to whiteness, and to commodification under neoliberal racial capitalism is troubling, to say the least. Not to mention how troubling is the co-optation of "Eastern" and other "ancient" practices, by a seemingly very *un*-self-aware white woman running a Tantra workshop on unceded Aztec land.

The Viral Expansion of the Self-Care Industrial Complex:
Effects on Global Political Economy

Goop gets a lot of attention—and a lot of critique and
fun poked its way.[34] But, as we've seen, it's not just Goop.
And it's possible that Goop has actually become a scape-
goat—a place to put all the blame for everything that's
wrong with elite, white, cis-feminized versions of self-
care. Denise Bedell, writing in 2018 for the website This
Is Capitalism says: "Increased interest in healthy living
and healthy lifestyle choices across different age segments
are driving the strong growth in the wellness sector . . .
this incredible growth story provides a solid foundation
for new business development, which women entrepreneurs are taking advantage of . . . but there are also a
number of other reasons why this sector works well as
a destination for female business owners." She goes on
to describe how women are "particularly well-suited to
lifestyle businesses," quoting Amanda Freeman, owner
of fitness chain SLT (Strength, Lengthen, Tone): "They
[women] want their work to be meaningful and enjoya-
ble . . . they're focused on healthy living themselves, so

---

34 In addition to Jen Gunter's now famous criticisms, Gabrielle
    Moss (2016), editor at *Bustle*, wrote an entire book as a Goop
    parody, entitled *Glop: Nontoxic, Expensive Ideas That Will Make
    You Look Ridiculous and Feel Pretentious.*

the transition from seeing wellness as not just a lifestyle but a business opportunity makes sense."

This (feminized) market logic is everywhere, and it resonates with many. It's not just espoused by the Goopy Gwyneth Paltrow that we all love to hate.

Comparative Religion scholar David Gordon White observes that the way Tantra is used in the Western sphere is a form of cultural appropriation.[35] He distinguishes neo-Tantra from Tantra in its original demonological and sexual magic tradition, in which sexual fluids are deemed to be power substances (sometimes the initiant will drink the seminal or uterine fluid of a teacher). White says: "Neo-Tantra is not Tantra, as it does not respect Tantra as it is described in the teaching found in the Tantric scriptures." This is a similar theme to what historian Jeff Wilson highlights when discussing Buddhist philosophy and mindful sex, as we mentioned in the previous chapter—in which a practice is divorced from its original framing, is appropriated, co-opted, and is ultimately used in a way that it was not intended for (sometimes being used in quite the opposite way).

---

35   White is interviewed in the second episode of the 2020 Netflix series *(Un)Well*, on "Tantric Sex," along with Sasha Cobra and Michaela Boehm. We draw from that interview here.

We don't think it's particularly helpful to argue for purity in terms of how any practice is or is not used, but we do think it is imperative to critically examine how these practices, well, *travel*—and the material, political, and economic consequences of that traveling. And often, this ideological appropriation has important material components.

When wealthy white people from the Global North travel to places around the globe as tourists in order to have "authentic cultural experiences" and "interact with local communities" this is how ideological appropriation is extended out into the world, with political economic consequences. Tantric sex retreat centers take up real space and have real environmental and economic effects on those spaces and the people who live there. And, in many of these places, working in the tourist industry then becomes the only option, which explains why wellness lifestyle real estate, the spa industry, and wellness tourism are some of the most lucrative up-and-coming sectors in the alternative health and wellness economy today. Further, many of the most invested extreme/transformational travelers make it clear that they want "authenticity," that they first-and-foremost desire to truly get a taste of "a different culture," and that they choose their wellness experiences with this in mind.

So: what is the answer here? Well, as mentioned at the end of the last chapter, we will explore some less exploitative, even decolonial possibilities for self-care in the Conclusion of this book. But, for now, it is worth mentioning that many organizers and activists have suggested some simple ways to begin the process of traveling and caring for one's self more thoughtfully, consciously, and responsibly.

For instance, *Yes!* magazine offers a list of tips for more equitable travel, including: sharing a meal in a local household, trading off hosting (use your own home to put up other travelers), lodging locally, spending intentionally (think local or fair trade), and touring responsibly (visit national parks, participate in homestays, and consider your carbon footprint at all times, of course).[36] These are all somewhat vague suggestions, but, hopefully, you get the point.

This is another thorny issue, as some would say traveling for holiday or vacation, insofar as it is part of tourism, is never okay (particularly for white people). In the last few decades, Black feminists have written some amazing and scathing critiques of the tourist industry, particularly of tourism in the Caribbean (we're thinking of Jamaica Kincaid and M. Jacqui Alexander among

---

36   Wafai, Larson, & Pucci (2019).

many brilliant others). Some say: "stay put." Of course, we want to get away from our homes and neighborhoods once in a while, just like everyone else does. But we are learning that there are ways to do this with impact and even justice in mind. One small step might be simply going somewhere closer; or, if you are going to travel somewhere with a particularly despicable tourist industry where there is already deep inequality and poverty, consider going somewhere else, or consider being very thoughtful about how you get there and what you do while you're there (and obviously do the research to shed light on these questions beforehand).

In terms of travel, tourism, real estate, and so many other pockets of the self-care market, women have been identified as a crucial consumer group, with newly garnered "spending power" that is ripe for harnessing. And women have been identified as important "early adopters" when it comes to new and up-and-coming trends in the wellness sector, and "innovators" of wellness and self-care business design (in terms of both *form* and *content*). But: who exactly are these *women*? What kind of *femininity* is it that is being branded as this new and exciting direction for capitalism? What kind of *feminism* are we talking about when femininity itself becomes a brand? And, most importantly, as we point to in the Introduction, which women are actually benefiting from this branding? And at which other women's (and people of all genders) expense?

Some have proposed that making the self-care industry accessible to more people—and, specifically, more non-white people—is the answer. For instance, in a 2021 article entitled "The Travel Industry's Reckoning with Race and Inclusion," Tariro Mzezwa describes how Black travelers and other tourists of color in the US are changing the face of the travel industry, by holding travel agencies' feet to the fire regarding their promises of inclusion in the wake of the racial justice protests of 2020. These tourists are choosing companies that seek to serve travelers of color, rather than just their usual wealthy, white base. And they are keen to support Black-owned travel businesses. There have also been calls to similarly ensure inclusion—and safety—for women and LGBTQ tourists.

In 2021, Ruchika Tulshyan interviewed Rachel Rodgers, author of a new book called *We Should All Be Millionaires*, for *The New York Times*. In the book, Rodgers thinks through how to ensure that Black women have more access to venture capital. According to Rodgers: "More non-white, non-male people should be earning seven figures." Her book is framed explicitly as a financial self-help guide that "focuses on earning more, building wealth and gaining economic power especially

among those who have traditionally been left out of the
high-income world like women of color, queer women
and disabled women." Rodgers' book is ultimately about
"how most financial advice excludes people of color,
how making more money requires women to first tap
into their desires, and how she reimagines capitalism so
that it benefits more than a handful." She says:

> Decades-old research finds that successful people
> are surrounded by other successful people. They
> have a powerful network. But you're not likely to
> have a powerful network if you grew up in a poor
> neighborhood, like I did. I had to really create my
> network . . . Ask yourself what *is it* I actually want.
> *Then* do the math on what it costs to get there . . .
> Eighty percent of women entrepreneurs never make
> more than $50,000 in total annual revenue. That is
> enraging. I was making six figures in my law practice
> and I did not feel like I'd "arrived" . . . If I could do
> it with the very limited resources that I had, every
> other woman of color can do it, too. And for those
> who truly can't, the rest of us need to do it so we can
> create opportunities for her.

Rodgers makes so many good points and we absolutely
agree with the importance of extending "financial literacy" to more diverse groups of people. However, we
also found ourselves cringing at the idea of "reimagin-
ing capitalism so that it benefits more than a handful"

presumably through providing more opportunities to access venture capital.

Diversity, equity, and inclusion—all keywords of our times—are incredibly important, for sure. But when considering the deeply unequal stakes of global capitalist destruction—of our environment and people's livelihoods—are diversity, equity, and inclusion or "DEI" initiatives (in the travel industry and financial literacy) enough? Or, put differently: are they enough to make the kinds of global political economic and structural changes that are so direly needed at this moment?

When do DEI efforts ultimately just perpetuate all of the pitfalls of (neo)liberal feminism? While simultaneously ignoring—or, even worse, re-entrenching— global colonialist structures?

Neoliberal Feminism, Woke Work, & Deep Inclusivity: The Promises and Pitfalls of DEI

We hope we have by now made a pretty convincing case that self-care has been brought into the capitalist fold in part via neoliberal feminism. Departing from earlier radical care practices, neoliberal feminists seek empowerment through the expansion of economic opportunities for women (sometimes even racially diverse women!) and advocate equality of opportunity, or women's access to "the same playing field" as men.

According to neoliberal feminism, global capitalism is not the root cause of inequality but rather a vehicle for achieving greater social parity. And ameliorating the hardships and traumas of ongoing inequality involves capturing the market. More specifically, the remedy entails *self-investment*—enhancing one's personal brand and one's well-being at the same time.

Emblematic of neoliberal feminism, self-care style, is the Global Wellness Initiative or GWI, a clearinghouse for information on the most cutting-edge health and wellness trends, and a kind of non-profit consortium NGO that supports wellness-oriented corporations (we have been citing data from their reports throughout this book; they are really very thorough and truly at the forefront of the self-care industrial complex!).

Every year, GWI puts on the "Global Wellness Summit," a kind of industry-wide conference, featuring pricey tickets, fancy selected delegates, and multiple levels of access (the 2021 conference was moved from Tel Aviv to Boston in light of the spread of the COVID-19 Delta Variant [we think?] but will be held in Tel Aviv in Fall 2022). Alongside the conference, a report is published to discuss what has been learned across the industry and what the newest fads are. The 2018 Global Wellness Summit's Global Wellness Trends Report outlines some of the lingo cropping up: "A new wave of feminism—a more political concept of self-care (less me, more us)—a growing realization that governments and medicine aren't hurrying to 'solve' for women's bodies and lives—means that . . . there are powerful new intersections between women's empowerment, feminism, and wellness . . . a new feminist wellness is rising, and it makes sense, as the wellness world has been quietly 'solving for women' for years."[37]

The authors of the report remark that this "women's-empowerment-meets-wellness-trend" makes sense insofar as "wellness has been very much a by women, for women, set of approaches." They mention that although "feminism" was the word of the year in 2017 according to Merriam-Webster, the terms "wellness" or "self-care" could easily have held the title instead. But these trendsetters lament that "wellness-*bashing*" could have been the runner-up, as "today, we see a vitriol against wellness seemingly more vocal than that against Tobacco or Big Pharma" due to the fact that the media loves to lampoon silly wellness celebs and the most self-indulgent, narcissistic, apolitical, elitist, and evidence-free of the wellness trends. This "wellness-bashing," the authors of the Report say, is unfortunate, however, given that "there is no greater medical evidence out there for

37   GWS (2018), p. 83.

anything than the impact that healthy eating, exercise, stress-reduction, sleep, and mental wellness have on human health." (Aww, poor corporate wellness trend-setters! Always being "bashed" . . . !)

However you slice it, it is undeniable that women have moved into the wellness industry as innovators, entrepreneurs, and practitioners, and they are taking an "empowered" stance in the sector (and all of its mini sectors). In some arenas, they are the majority shareholders.

Citing the surge in women-only clubs and co-working spaces (for women of "diverse" political ideologies!), a boom in "FemTech" and other smart solutions for the embodied problems women face, and a new entourage of female leadership in everything from human resources or HR for workplace wellness programs to online sex toy stores to clothing companies, wellness trend experts make the case that women's economic power within a capitalist marketplace *is feminist*—categorically. And the revamped industries and markets that these new "fourth wave"[38] feminists are creating—or, at the very least, influencing—take

---

38 GWS (2018), pp. 92-93: The report describes some of the key elements of "our fourth wave of feminism" moment: "wilder and tougher, less orthodox and more creative, a little less about me than we, and where, whether feminism is or is not a proud political tag you wear, it's still essentially your lifestyle choice."

"deep inclusivity" and a "thrive revolution" at work very seriously. Regarding this "workplace wellness revolution," the GWI's Global Wellness Economy Monitor reports: "As we look to the future, conversations around wellness at work will no longer center on mitigating work-related ills, but on enhancing motivation, commitment, creativity, flow, cognitive abilities, etc.—in other words, thriving at work." Wow.

What does it mean to "thrive" at work? Well, key elements of this thriving workplace are said to include:

1) "the well-being of WE" (employers' recognition that "thriving" is core to sustainable success, and a thriving work culture is key to attracting and retaining talent),

2) a "purpose-driven workplace and conscious evolution of leadership" (emphasis on the need to "[re]build trust between business and society"),

3) "mental wellness and individualized well-being" (a focus on fostering happiness, generativity, effectiveness, and wisdom at work via DNA and other biomarker testing and cognitive technologies for behavior change, etc. to boost brain activity, reduce stress, and increase productivity), and, of particular interest to us for this book—

4) "women-friendly" workplaces and "deep inclusivity" (women-friendly workplaces are said to bring "a focus on diversity, the challenges of care-giving, pay inequities, ageism, and other well-being concerns that can particularly plague women . . . [that] harnessing all talent requires deep inclusion . . . and research suggests that true diversity and inclusion will produce more innovative, engaged, and high-performing teams; increase profitability; enhance brand appeal; and attract talent").

Although the "thrive revolution" at work is billed as being about the need for "a high-trust environment of mutual respect and psychological safety," it is first and foremost about improving "shared outcomes" (between employers and workers)—or, rather, a "shared" investment in sales, profit, and the bottom line.

A far cry from the revolutionary feminist protocol of living room self-cervical-exams and justice-seeking care collectives, this is neoliberal feminism in the flesh.

Care here, you may have noticed, is completely compatible with the almighty dollar.

If "diversity," "equity," and "inclusion" are keywords today, then so is "empowerment," or, more frequently, "*self*-empowerment." And #thefutureisfemale,

#smashthepatriarchy, #nevertheslessshepersisted, and #nastywomenunite are key hashtags, especially in the post-2017 Women's March and post-#MeToo milieu.

Notably, an emphasis on "deep inclusivity" also means that these new health and wellness-focused companies are not only making space for the women who are taking the wellness sector by storm, but that the women who are doing so can no longer be assumed to be only white—these companies foreground safety and transformation for *all* women. GWI states:

> If #WellnessSoWhite has been a disturbing reality (if sometimes overstated [sic!]), we're seeing entrepreneurial women of color jump in to solve for women of color: whether with new for-them fitness or yoga classes or beauty brands rolling out cosmetic lines to suit dozens of skin tones. More wellness travel will be squarely aimed at women's empowerment: whether safe extreme adventure travel for the solo woman— more retreats for women to heal emotionally (like post-divorce/break-up retreats) or those that help women get their sexual wellness back or are inventing much more women-empowering beauty programs.[39]

Within today's neoliberal feminism, self-empowerment incorporates diversity and is sometimes even multiracial. But women of color are first and foremost conceived as an

39   GWS (2018), pp. 83-84.

important market and spending base, and only secondly are they celebrated as entrepreneurs, influencers, or, in a few cases, as founders.

Black women-owned yoga studios, for instance, like Black Girl OM in Chicago, or the global woman-owned company OMNoire, which holds expensive sold-out retreats in Granada, are often praised for turning the tides of the whiteness epidemic in the wellness industry and for making self-care more diverse and accessible for all: "#WellnessSoWhite has [highlighted] a serious problem with representation, even though spa, beauty, travel and fitness companies know firsthand that women of color are very passionate about self-care and a powerful customer base . . . [soon] we'll see more entrepreneurial women of color solve for women of color . . . and we'll see more women of color become more visible and powerful in wellness generally, whether as fitness influencers or company founders—remaking wellness as a much less white space."[40]

As we mentioned earlier regarding "BFF marketing," often, women-owned companies and firms emphasize the "brand story" of the woman founder, along with an "empowering message"—and this technique is celebrated as it helps to foster emotional attachments to the

40   GWS (2018), pp. 90-91.

brand. Women's empowerment and even activism are thus part of marketing schemes. Take, for instance, the trend of women-only social clubs, wellness collectives, and co-working spaces. Founders Audrey Gelman and Lauren Kassan of New York City-based The Wing[41] (the "boss-lady" social club that is "non-partisan" in terms of political ideology, where private memberships cost up to $3,000 per year, and which currently has a 9,000+ woman waiting list) describe it as "a coven, not a sorority" and "a place for women on their way." The founders of the "coven" further characterize their own operating principles as "career and racial and ethnic diversity" and state that they're both "unapologetically capitalist *and* activist." Yikes.

The 2018 GWS Trends Report ends by firmly and clearly bringing together these ideas about the new "deep inclusivity": "The recent feminist wave has spurred this wave of for-women, by-women wellness . . . but feminist climate or not in the future, this trend all comes down to one powerful, undeniable fact: the sheer global growth in women's spending power (and education and

---

41   For an in-depth discussion of The Wing and an investigation into its not-so-woman-friendly (and racist) labor practices, see Hess (2020). For more on how Black and Brown women workers at The Wing eventually pushed Audrey Gelman to step down as CEO, see Rosman (2020).

knowledge power)—with nearly all leading economic thinkers agreeing the financial and economic *future is female* [italics added]."

"Feminism" here is thus equated with access and power in the capitalist marketplace—and, of course, everyone deserves a seat at the table. But what do multiple seats at the table for a (slightly) more diverse cohort of elite women from the Global North actually offer in terms of providing *real care* for the many around the world who need it, and who regularly provide it for others? How might we distinguish neoliberal *multi*racial capitalism from a serious anti-racist and decolonial care praxis?

The neoliberal feminism of today and the self-help feminism of the 1970s are not quite the same, then (even though they do have things in common). The self-help feminism of times past, even as it was imperfectly inter-sectional, too often gynocentric, and inadequate in its considerations of class, *was* invested in a radical and rev-olutionary protocol—and a seriously different "how-to" guide for living and caring. The process and the practice were political, and the way things were done mattered (for example, the cervical exam could, without a doubt, be performed in a "more feminist way," and how it was performed mattered—who was performing it mattered, as well). If, under neoliberal feminism today, "deep inclusivity" in the workplace and marketplace is the new protocol, have the practice and process really changed? In fact, today's protocol centers spending power and marketing prowess, and who is driving the market is what appears to matter most. And this does nothing to alter—let alone eradicate—global systems of coloniality, inequality, and structural violence.

Regardless of how deep it actually goes, something is at least *understood* to be different about inclusivity when it is "deep" and #thefutureisfemale. But: isn't this all just good-for-business sloganeering? Is there any chance it's the result of a hard-fought battle won by actual social movements? We have our doubts that it is evidence of any kind of real change (seems more like rebranded soft-and-gentle capitalism to us, to be perfectly honest)—but the tension itself is most certainly at the heart of our current self-care moment.

We will come back to these questions and continue to address them in the Conclusion. For now, we turn to self-care fads in the world of food, diets, and functional medicine, where we see many of the same problems and pitfalls playing out.

Chapter 3

YOU CAN NOURISH YOUR FAMILY AND CLIMB THE LADDER OF SUCCESS! THE WHITE NEOLIBERAL FEMINISM AND HIP DOMESTICITY OF FOOD-BASED HEALTH MOVEMENTS

Years ago, one of us was sitting in on a workshop led by a health coach. The health coach worked for a major wellness and weight loss company, which shall remain nameless (though trust us—you've heard of them). Addressing the audience, the coach said that she loved to see the look on the new faces in the crowd as they really took in the benefits of the program. She said that the "look" was one of hope. She then went on to say "I believe that's what [company] sells. Our biggest product is hope." It's almost certain that this health coach made that comment with full sincerity; she really seemed to be a true believer! But the irony in her words was too much. So much so that the one of us who was sitting in the audience that afternoon actually took out a pen and paper and wrote that quote down . . .

We tell you this story because it gets at the heart of why so many of us find ourselves reading websites, social media posts, and books on improving our health; buying exercise or kitchen equipment (that we have every intention of using at the time); and trying various health improvement treatments, supplements, and classes. Maybe we're worried that something is wrong. Maybe we just feel like things could be better than they are. Regardless of what sends us to Google or social media apps or Amazon in search of answers and remedies—at the bottom of it all is hope. And of all the health topics we go online in search of, food and diet are paramount amongst them.

But what answers do we find there?

We Don't Know What the Hell Gluten Is, But We're Pretty Sure It's Bad for Us

It was 2014 and gluten-free as a lifestyle choice was starting to take off. Poking a little fun at what appeared to be the latest food craze, late-night television host Jimmy Fallon had his crew interview people about gluten at a local Los Angeles exercise spot. All of the respondents indicated that they avoided gluten in their lives for health and weight-loss reasons, but not one could define what it was (to be fair, the footage might have been edited to suggest just this very thing, leaving out those who could define it accurately). Fallon remarked that he too had not known what gluten (proteins found in wheat and a number of other grains) was, but that in Los Angeles, it was tantamount to satanism.

The year before Fallon aired this segment of his show, 30 percent of Americans reported that they had reduced or eliminated gluten in their diets.[42] In 2013 and 2014, paleo was the most Googled diet while keto was ranked by Google as the most popular diet in 2018. A recent *Business Insider* poll found that the most popular diet that millennials expressed interest in trying was one that is low-carbohydrate. Relatedly, according to a *Fortune* poll, more than 36 percent of respondents had tried a low- or no-carbohydrate diet. Yet, only about 1 percent of the population contends with celiac disease. So why are so many people avoiding gluten, and more broadly, eating low-carb?

Many gluten-free adherents have self-diagnosed as suffering from non-celiac gluten sensitivity (NCGS) or other gluten-/grain-related food allergies. Others have based their decisions to adhere to a gluten-free diet (GFD) on the results of direct-to-consumer (DTC) food sensitivity blood tests. Notably, debate remains in the medical literature as to whether or not NCGS is clinically legitimate. As well, DTC food sensitivity blood

42   For more on the food and food industry trends reported in this section, see: American Academy of Allergy, Asthma, & Immunology (n.d.); Chang & Nowel (2016); DiGiacomo, et al. (2013); Freudenberg (2014); Gaesser & Angadi (2012); Gans (2019); Kotecki (2019); Kowitt (2015); Larocca (2017); Lis, et al. (2014); Moore (2014); Newberry, et al. (2017); Strom (2014); Taparia & Koch (2015); and Tavakkoli, et al. (2014).

tests are also held by allergists and immunologists to be lacking in scientific validity. Nevertheless, gluten-free low-carbohydrate (GFLC) advocates seem to feel passionately that these dietary regimens result in the alleviation of symptoms, the resolution of ill health, and enhancement of vitality and well-being.

But GFLC diets aren't just popular; they have become big business. Keep in mind that compared to other sectors, the food industry relies on the release of a steady stream of new products in order to generate profits. Each year, the food sector introduces over 20,000 new food products into global markets, a twenty-fold uptick since 1970. And so it is not surprising that in response to rising interest in GFD and GFLC diets, there has been a tremendous expansion of gluten-free, paleo, and Whole30 (a more restrictive variation of the paleo diet) certified products available for purchase, as well. Between 2004 and 2011, the gluten-free market grew by 28 percent. Today, some estimates value this market at $15 billion worldwide.

Related to the rising interest in GFLC diets is a broader interest in "clean eating." This term refers to the notion of eating fresh, unprocessed foods to enhance health and well-being. It also often refers to eating non-genetically modified (non-GMO), organic foods, and in some versions, it may include eating raw foods and/or minimizing or avoiding grains and sometimes animal products. While GFLC diets such as paleo, Whole30, and autoimmune paleo (an even *more* restrictive variation on the paleo diet) can be said to fall under the larger umbrella of "clean eating," there are also obvious differences between these versions and those that advocate veganism as the ultimate form of eating clean.

Regardless of what one eats and what one avoids, the assertion that some foods and some ways of eating are "clean" has been criticized as elitist in that other foods must therefore be "dirty" (and perhaps by extension, so are those who eat them). Notably, the types of foods lauded by clean eating proponents are far more expensive than their processed options, as we will discuss later in this chapter.

Clean eating has had a similar impact as GFLC on markets. Between 2009 and 2014 "big food" lost roughly 18 billion in sales, as shoppers increasingly avoided the center of the supermarket where processed foods are typically found and gravitated toward the perimeter to buy fresh food. In fact, sales of fresh prepared foods have grown nearly 30 percent in the past decade. Also, organic food sales more than tripled between 2004 and 2014. Relatedly, sales of commercially prepared baby food have been declining for more than a decade as parents made their own baby food or purchased organic varieties in greater numbers. According to the same *Fortune* poll mentioned earlier, more than three quarters of respondents are trying to eat healthier; nearly 65 percent of shoppers are very or extremely concerned about pesticides; and more than 85 percent believe that genetically modified foods should be labeled. Finally, roughly 42 percent of millennials report a lack of trust in major food companies.

Meet the New Natural Diet, Same as the Old Natural Diet? (A Very Brief History)

The advocacy of eating in specific ways for the purposes of avoiding or curing illness and enhancing health, wellness, and vitality is nothing new. In Western societies, connections between food and health are said to go back to Hippocrates in the fifth century B.C.[43]

But let's flash forward a bit. Regardless of whether or not we hit those center supermarket food aisles when we go grocery shopping, in the United States certainly we've at least heard of "Graham Crackers" and Kellogg's

---

43   On the history of natural food diets as discussed here, see: Cardenas (2013); Laurdan (2001); Levenstein (2012); and Martin (2003).

brand cereals. Interestingly, the early-nineteenth-century Reverend Sylvester Graham did not invent Graham Crackers. Rather, they were created by his followers, who took up his teachings on health, food, and morality. The good Reverend was an early American advocate of natural foods, prepared at home (obviously, by women). Processed foods, he argued, not only went against God's laws of health, but they also contributed to the debilitation of health, in part by stimulating the urge to masturbate in young people (maybe that one made more sense at the time?). One of Graham's disciples, John Harvey Kellogg, condemned white flour and refined sugar as unnatural—though not, ironically, in the cereal products that he himself created!

Advocates of natural, unprocessed foods faded into the background in the early twentieth century, as large food processors were praised for bringing nutritious and safer (hello: delayed spoilage!) foods to increasing numbers of the American public. Still, ideas about healthier, more simple ways of eating continued to find resonance throughout the twentieth century.

For example, in the 1930s, the British colonial physician Sir Robert McCarrison, who was part of the Indian Medical Service, "discovered" that the "uncivilized" Himalayan Hunza people seemed to suffer from none of the ailments that plagued the "civilized" westerners. Attributing their health and longevity to their natural, unprocessed diet, McCarrison's take on the Hunza would later inspire other western authors and filmmakers for decades to come (the good ol' exotic, mystical primitive trope never gets old, apparently . . .). One such individual was Jerome Irving Cohen (who later changed his last name to Rodale). Rodale wrote the highly popular book *The Healthy Hunza* and later founded popular magazines such as *Organic Farming and Gardening* and *Prevention*.

In the mid- to late twentieth century, both the avoidance of foods with additives, preservatives, and crops grown in a conventional manner and eating "naturally" were taken up by the 1960s and 1970s hippie and New Left movements. These movements advocated for (amongst many other things) self-sufficiency in health as a means by which to wrest control from mistrusted institutions such as government and industry. By the late 1970s, a majority of the American public believed natural food was the healthier and safer option, and the food industry noticed, seeing the claim of "natural" as a powerful marketing tactic. In fact, by 1977, over 25 percent of advertisements in women's magazines specifically pertained to the importance of the "natural" for health and well-being.

Quite distinct from these previous iterations was the very-low-carbohydrate diet popularized by Dr. Robert Atkins, who began publishing books on the benefits of his diet for weight loss in the 1970s. Though Atkins did not advocate a return to simpler, more natural ways of eating, he did suggest that avoiding carbohydrates would lead to weight loss and better health. Moreover, his medical practice was one that combined allopathic (biomedical) care with complementary and alternative medicine techniques.

Today's "clean eating" diets are less (explicitly) oriented around weight loss and more around a return to a more "natural" way of eating for the purposes of health. Yet like the different health movements of the past, today's health-improvement diets have a common basis in (white) middle-class fears and anxieties (as discussed in the Introduction to this book). They also have a grounding in frustrations with, if not outright distrust of, many status-quo institutions such as the health care system, the food sector, the pharmaceutical industry, and the federal government. Finally, they often traffic in romanticized (and we would argue *colonial*) notions of "simpler times" when humans were allegedly freed from the rat-race and more in tune with nature. This includes diets that are said to be more in line with "ancestral" ways of eating and alternative healing practices. And this is what we turn to next.

Functional Medicine: How Unconventional Is It Really?

Perhaps given the contestation over non-celiac gluten sensitivity and (some) autoimmune conditions, adherents to GFLC diets have often looked outside of biomedical care for information and advice, frequently to alternative health practitioners. Such practitioners are held to be more trustworthy than allopathic providers, who are believed to be too closely tied to the pharmaceutical industry. Naturopathy, in essence, entails a belief in the body's own natural healing abilities when such abilities are enhanced by the avoidance of certain foods, the uptake of others, detoxification, supplementation, and other lifestyle changes. It is a holistic healing modality that follows a personalized approach. "Functional medicine," which is closely aligned with GFLC diets, includes naturopathic approaches but also integrates aspects of allopathy.

In functional medicine, the body is viewed as a dynamic system with both health and disease resulting from the interactions of biology and environmental exposures (generally defined as factors such as diet, lifestyle, microbes, allergens, environmental toxins, social connections, and stressors). By seeing the body in this manner, advocates of the functional medicine approach claim that they work *with* the body by getting to the root of disease and ill health instead of treating ailments in a piecemeal approach and suppressing symptoms with drugs and surgeries. Many functional medicine practices combine practitioners trained in allopathy (such as doctors and nurses) who take a functional medicine approach, with those trained in complementary and alternative medicine (such as acupuncturists and naturopaths), and health coaches, thus offering "the best of both worlds."

In order to understand some of the key tenets (and limitations) of functional medicine in its current form, take the work of Chris Kresser. Kresser operates a functional medicine practice in collaboration with other providers as well as a functional medicine training institute. Chief amongst the many benefits of the functional medicine paradigm for both patients and providers alike, according to Kresser, is that functional medicine is a "leaner operation" resulting in more of a "high touch" approach. What he means by this is that by operating independently, outside the world of health insurance reimbursement, and by combining both in-person and virtual appointments, providers reduce overhead costs.

By reducing these costs, they have a more flexible practice, can see fewer patients per day, have time to keep up with the latest research, and can offer longer appointments and more personalized care. Though some bloodwork and testing may be covered by patients' health insurance plans or work health savings accounts, ultimately functional medicine providers operate on a fee-for-service basis.

Kresser offers another reason for operating on a fee-for-service basis—the motivations of insurance companies themselves. The interests of insurance companies are not well aligned with the nation's health, he suggests, in that they earn their profits through expanding health care costs (which, in turn, result from exploding chronic disease). When providers rely on an insurance reimbursement system, they are limited to offering only those forms of treatment that will be covered by insurers.

While Kresser's critique that the profit motivations of insurance companies limit the provision of treatment and care in the United States is certainly on target, ironically, he also notes that adopting a functional medicine practice can increase the revenue potential *for functional medicine providers themselves.*

Kresser acknowledges that in the short-term, offering care in such a manner may put functional medicine financially out of reach for many, and he suggests solutions such as sliding scale services, discounts for low-income clients, and group wellness classes, which are more affordable than one-on-one coaching. Still, he maintains, by focusing on disease prevention, in the long-term, functional medicine is the more affordable choice for both individuals and the nation at large. Kresser argues, "Patients may have to increase the amount of money they initially invest in their health, understanding that, like other good investments, they'll receive a significant return over time."

If this sounds elitist (Gallup Polls consistently find that only slightly over half of the American public owns stocks) and like a very short-sighted means by which to address inefficiencies and inequities in the nation's health care system, that's because it is.

Consider Parsley Health, the boutique functional medicine service we mentioned in the last chapter, who provides care to those who can afford to "invest upfront." Founded by medical doctor and tech entrepreneur Robin Berzin, Parsley Health has in-person operations in major cities around the United States and offers virtual appointments for clients outside of those areas. For $150 *per month*, members get five visits with a doctor per year, five sessions with a health coach to help ensure the member follows the recommended health protocols, and unlimited app messaging with coaches and providers. What they term "advanced biomarker testing" has a separate cost outside of the monthly membership (as do other services and treatments such as prescribed supplements).

Notably, Parsley Health does not accept insurance. However, as with Kresser, Parsley Health is sure to note on its website that members may be able to use health savings accounts to cover the cost of their plans, treatments, and tests.

Just Like Our Paleolithic Ancestors Used to Eat: A Just-So Story

In functional medicine as well as GFLC diets, the main routes to good health and healing (and conversely the main routes to ill health) are said to pertain to lifestyle factors, most particularly diet. As Melissa and Dan Hartwig, originators of the Whole30 diet claim in their foundational book, *It Starts with Food*, "The food you eat either makes you more healthy or less healthy. Those are your options." Well, that certainly simplifies things!

In paleo and paleo-related diets such as Whole30 and autoimmune paleo, gluten and grains are held to be toxic to the body. Popularized by health scientist

Loren Cordain, paleo diet proponents argue that the human genome has not had sufficient time to adapt to the introduction of agriculture (e.g., grains and dairy), which has resulted in an evolutionary mismatch between what we eat and our physiological processes. The result has been an explosion of chronic disease. Thus, a return to more "ancestral" ways of eating—avoidance of all grains, legumes, and dairy—is understood to be a key path to health. (Can't you just picture it? Paleolithic families huddled around the fire frying up their almond-flour-battered, grass-fed bison in first cold-pressed, organic avocado oil . . . !).

For the authors of the 2018 *Global Wellness Summit* (GWS) "Global Wellness Trends Report," things went wrong with regard to food and health (and, apparently, gender roles) a bit more recently. During World War II, when women were called to take the place of men in the factories, home cooking suffered. The authors write: "Processed foods, microwave meals, and TV dinners filled the void left by an absent housewife who could no longer spend hours a day preparing meals from scratch." Why make home-cooked meals with fresh ingredients, they ask, when one could quickly reheat a "family" (they put this word in quotes) meal to be shared in front of the television?

Though there is no question that increasingly processed foods changed the diets and eating habits of individuals and families, we really have to take issue with the notion that "absent housewives" were the root cause of these shifts. Moreover, working class and women of color had long been working outside the home, often *in* the homes of well-off white women. The shifts that the GWS authors discuss were limited to a very select group of households. As well, some historians have argued that processed foods were *welcomed* by women as they freed them from toiling in the kitchen and reduced spoilage, stretching a family's food budget. [44]

What you should be picking up on here is that the relationship between food, health, and illness is often related in the form of a "just-so" story, or a story told about the past that is used to explain a phenomenon in the present—one that would be difficult (if not impossible) to test. Though archaeological records provide some evidence, we can't exactly go back in time and interview

44   For a much more nuanced historical discussion of early
     twentieth century changes in the American diet, particularly in
     relation to gendered norms and expectations, see Deutch (2010);
     Laurdan (2001); and Miller (2020). See Knight (2015) for more
     on the ways in which some low-carb dieters reconstruct the
     evolutionary past in order to justify contemporary choices while
     others challenge these reconstructions.

a bunch of paleolithic-era individuals about what they are eating and why . . . To be fair, some paleo and functional medicine proponents are careful to point out that the evolutionary record isn't quite so clear and that hunter-gatherer groups ate a variety of foods, depending on the area of the world from which they hailed.

Beyond references to what paleolithic people supposedly did or didn't eat, what evidence do GFLC proponents base their health claims on? The answer seems to be a mix of anecdotal experience and scientific evidence. Open up many of the bestselling GFLC books and cookbooks (as well as websites) and you may find another sort of story—a story of redemption (I once was lost but now am found). That is, the author references having suffered in a prolonged manner from an assortment of ailments but having gotten no relief (nor a proper diagnosis) from biomedical providers. The author then describes frustrated and sometimes desperate searches for effective treatments, trying one method after another, but to no avail (and if the author is a medical provider themself, the discussion is more about the frustrations of not being able to offer patients effective treatment). Eventually, whichever diet is being promoted is discovered, adopted, and then becomes a form of salvation.

And the benefits ascribed to clean/ancestral diets in these stories don't just stop at the alleviation of physiological symptoms and the resolution of physical health concerns. Rather, these benefits also extend to other forms of well-being. For instance, *Nom Nom Paleo* author Michelle Tam writes that after becoming paleo, her energy levels shot up, she lost weight, and she had enough energy to not only hold down her graveyard shift job as a pharmacist, but also parent two young boys, hit the gym hard, and develop and maintain a bestselling app and blog. The Hartwigs, in describing the benefits of the Whole30 diet as reported to them by their clients and followers, suggest that it results in high energy, better sleep, improved endurance, increased mental acuity, improved digestion, and even a "sunnier disposition."

But lest we think that these are merely subjective claims, GFLC proponents also reference the scientific basis for the diets they promote. Those who have medical or scientific credentials are sure to mention them (sometimes repeatedly). Some state that the basis of their work rests upon years (or decades) of both clinical experience *and* immersion in the scientific literature.

The Hartwigs, for example, let the reader know they are bringing "the best of both worlds" to their work—that is: years of carefully examining the science and years of "boots-on-the-ground" experience working with Whole30 adherents. This combination, they argue, is a "win-win." But, they continue, the true test of the diet's efficacy is user experience. That is, undertaking the Whole30 gives each individual the opportunity to conduct a thirty-day self-experiment on their specific food triggers, something that clinical trials and observational studies cannot provide, they state, because investigators have not included *each of us* in said trials and research. (True. And also not how clinical trials work, as the authors surely know . . .) This is proclaimed a "win-win-win."

We acknowledge that it makes sense that individuals promoting (selling) a specific way of *eating* would emphasize *diet* as a cause of health and illness in their work. Moreover, we don't wish to diminish or disparage real experiences of suffering. (We have experienced firsthand the limitations and failures of allopathic medicine to address many health conditions. We also regularly consume non-glutinous flour, kale, and coconut milk . . .) We fundamentally believe in embodied knowledge and the grassroots activism of contested illness sufferers. And we recognize both the benefits *and limits* of the scientific method. Our quarrel is not so much with these aspects of clean/ancestral eating proponents' arguments; rather, it is with the narrow and myopic ways in which clean/ancestral eating and functional medicine promoters discuss the causes of and solutions to widespread health concerns.

These proponents often emphasize factors beyond just food as a cause of and solution to ill health. So, what are these factors? Kresser states that the functional medicine approach combines a paleo diet ("ancestral eating"), physical activity, meaningful social connection, adequate sleep, and a healthy balance of work and play (regarding the latter, he states that hunter-gatherer societies worked only three to four hours a day, much of which was carried out in a social context and was not compulsive. Sounds great—sign us up!). Read the opening chapter of many GFLC books and cookbooks and you'll find a similar list. But these too are framed as *lifestyle* factors—or factors held to be under a reasonable degree of individual control.

Consider the words of Alaena Haber and Sarah Ballantyne, the authors of an AIP cookbook *The Healing Kitchen:* "It's easy to feel that our own health is beyond our control—we blame our genetics or our environment, we say it runs in our family, our doctors tell us it's just bad luck and that no one knows why one person gets a particular disease while the next one remains healthy.

But in truth, we do have control: our health is almost entirely within our power to change and improve. And it starts when we make one healthy choice at a time."

Often, economic barriers to access aren't addressed at all. For instance, the authors of the GWS 2018 trend report claim "while organic goods typically cost more than foods grown with chemicals and fertilizers, consumers *don't mind* paying more for these products" (emphasis added). The authors further suggest that the expansion of organic markets is due to the fact that consumers now "*care more* about the freshness and quality of their food" (again, emphasis added because, wow). Presumably, then, those who do not buy organic don't care about these issues?!

Those authors who do address the economic barriers associated with the higher cost of GFLC diets (let alone ones based on organic foods, pastured and grass-fed meats, and wild seafood) tend to highlight the fact that budget shopping can be done, if one gets creative. Economic barriers are sometimes also portrayed, a la Kresser, as a necessary cost of moving the nation to a true system of health and healing. Yet, addressing the larger, macro-level, structural factors which determine health and disease and moreover health disparities, is rare to see in these texts.

To the extent that broader factors are acknowl-
edged, the discussion tends to be about particular industries. Kresser says that the insurance industry is focused
more on profit than on improving health outcomes.
Grain Brain keto diet author Dr. David Perlmutter suggests that the pharmaceutical industry profits when we
remain unwell as it creates a demand for their products.
And a common refrain is that "food just isn't what it
used to be." Indeed, instead of offering us whole, fresh
foods, the food sector does make profits by creating
highly palatable—even addictive—processed foods
that offer little in the way of nutrition (this is true, by
the way). City University of New York Distinguished
Professor of Public Health Nicholas Freudenberg states
that they do so by exploiting the fact that salt, fat, and
sugar were relatively rare for hunter-gatherer societies
and thus humans tended to heavily consume foods with
these attributes when they could be found. These processed foods also contain chemical additives to enhance
flavor and mouthfeel.

Some authors point to the influence "Big Food"
has over the United States Department of Agriculture's
(USDA) nutritional guidelines. Dr. Mark Hyman, an
originator of the functional medicine approach, points
to the limitations of nutrition science, which focuses

on examining dietary components in isolation. This approach, says Hyman, fails to capture the way in which these dietary components interact with one another as well as with complex human biochemistry. It is, however, useful to the food industry, which can use this form of nutrition science to market a given product as high in a particular vitamin or mineral, or otherwise "healthy" in some way. We don't disagree with any of these critiques. The problem is that when these factors are mentioned in clean/ancestral and functional medicine writings, they often take a backseat to the discussion of lifestyle factors.

And, in this sense, these clean/ancestral and functional medicine authors offer very little in the way of a true challenge to the status quo. Rather, their work fits perfectly into existing raced, classed, gendered, and neocolonial structures of power and inequality.

Leisured, Chic, Serene (and Alive)

In Ira Levin's classic book *The Stepford Wives,* the protagonist, Johanna Eberhart, becomes suspicious of the too-perfect lives and regressive gender politics of the Connecticut suburb to which she and her husband have moved. Eberhart, a feminist, is dismayed to learn that many of the women in Stepford had given up their careers and/or women's rights organizing in order to focus on caring for their husbands and children in the home. When she enquires about their choices to do so, time and time again the answer is the same: domestic labor is a better use of a woman's time and far more fulfilling. In expressing her concerns to a confidant, Eberhart notes that she went to get her hair done in a nearby town of Norwood and there, she saw women who were "rushed and sloppy and irritated and alive." The Norwood women were quite unlike the perfectly coiffed, docile wives in Stepford, who happily, endlessly, and blissfully labored on behalf of their families without so much as a hair out of place. Eberhart is so overtaken with relief in seeing the women of Norwood that she wanted to "hug every one of them." As a satirical novel, Levin is poking some fun at the 1950s *Father Knows Best* white, middle-class, cis-heteronormative, suburban fantasy, one that was dependent, of course, on the exploited labor of working-class people, particularly people of color.

But what does *The Stepford Wives* have to do with contemporary food-based health advocacy? As with sellers of "mindful sex" and all things Goop, in many ways, contemporary "clean" and "ancestral" eating books, blogs, and social media pages traffic in an upgraded version of this same fantasy.

Many of the bloggers and Instagrammers who have made a name (and an income) for themselves through the advocacy of clean/ancestral eating seem to be relatively young, thin, white, cis women whose self-care brands reflect an elite white femininity and gender essentialism. Neither docile, programmed, and robotic (like the women of Stepford) nor rushed, sloppy, and irritated (like the women of Norwood), these individuals appear leisured, chic, serene, *and* alive, thanks to the self-care lifestyle changes that they have made and now promote. In this sense, we agree with the journalist Jordan Kisner who argues that the contemporary version of self-care in the US seems driven by an online performance of already privileged white women demonstrating their flawless success in Zen-like wellness as an entrepreneurial project.

An interesting theme found throughout clean/ancestral eating blogs, social media pages, and cookbooks is that while the women who run them find a measure of economic success in doing so, they highlight the importance of their work nurturing and nourishing their husbands and children. "Nourish" is a word commonly part of the clean/ancestral diet milieu. In fact, many describe their families as a primary motivation for having made clean/ancestral lifestyle changes: that is, they wanted to heal themselves from chronic illness in order to be more available to their families and/or because they want to ensure their families' own health and well-being.[45]

Consider the proliferation of "mama"-monikered clean/ancestral and alternative health blogs. Many of these women are not just bloggers but their sites and posts contain sponsored content, promotions, and many have authored books and cookbooks and host podcasts. These blogs can be seen as a subset of the parenting blogosphere, and the authors as a subset of mommy bloggers. Bringing together social media, alternative health, clean/ancestral eating, and essentialist notions of gender, they focus on natural health and nutrition, as well as other "lifestyle" content.

Examples include the blogs: Don't Mess with Mama, The Mommypotamus, The Paleo Mama, The Coconut

45 The Global Wellness Summit (GWS, 2018) states that the "wellness kitchen of the future" (one that we note would be, based on the description and mock-ups, accessible only to those at the highest income levels), "serves as a sanctuary, not a pressure cooker" (p. 38). The authors of the report state that in the wellness kitchen of the future "everyone is a chef, and everyone contributes to meal preparation and serving" (pg. 41). Thus, presumably there will be more equitable division of domestic labor in cis-heterosexual households in the future (we certainly hope so). With that said, there are only two photographs featured in this section of the GWS report—one of a family eating together and one of an individual smiling while preparing a meal—an individual who appears to be a cis woman (pp. 43 & 46).

Mama, The Paleo Running Momma, The Paleo Mom, and The Wellness Mama, just to name a handful. (We have yet to find equivalent GFLC "daddy" blogs.) With some exceptions, these blogs are replete with wholesome "all-American" looking photos of white, middle-class families. In the "About" section of their sites, one finds that the bloggers typically identify as "moms" first, "wives" second, and from there, often mention their paid careers and/or identities as writers.

Of note is the ways in which these women frame their clean/ancestral and self-care journeys. For instance, the blogger who runs Don't Mess with Mama writes, "Both my husband and oldest son have battled health issues for years without a real answer from conventional medicine. No one took their health issues seriously. But a mother (and wife) knows in her gut when something is wrong."[46] Similarly, the titular blogger for The Wellness Mama is described in the following manner, "A mom of six with a background in journalism, she took health into her own hands and started researching to find answers to her own health struggles."

---

46   The updated version of the blog no longer contains this exact
     language; however, the original text can be found via the
     Wayback Machine: https://web.archive.org/web/
     20190222125423/https://dontmesswithmama.com/about/.

And, perhaps most interestingly, The Paleo Mom, aka Dr. Sarah Ballantyne, a biophysicist and medical researcher by training (as well as arguably one of the top—if not *the* top—autoimmune paleo authors), asserts that she is "more than just a scientist." Her bio continues, "She is also a devoted mom and wife. It was important to Dr. Sarah to improve the health of her family in addition to addressing her own health conditions."

In their writings, many (though not all, e.g., Ballantyne) of these bloggers reject mainstream medical and parenting advice, which they see as suspect or even corrupt, and instead rely upon intuition that derives from their status as wives and mothers as well as their own embodied knowledge in order to make health and nutrition decisions for their families. Such bloggers often point to the toxicity of our current society, noting that it is out of touch with nature and, in some cases, God. However, instead of advocating for structural reforms to better advance the health of all families, they focus on what sociologist Jennifer Reich describes as "individualist parenting." Specifically, they tend to emphasize the importance of practices such as clean/ancestral diets, natural healing, extended breastfeeding, homeschooling, and even homesteading as a means by which to avoid risk and promote the health (and, by extension, life chances) of one's own family.

The subtext of this work is that a return to health is a return to nature, a hip form of domesticity and self-sufficiency, and an effective way to climb the ladder of success.

Certainly, we acknowledge the very real, ongoing, gendered expectations regarding care, health, and domestic labor, and we do not wish to engage in more mother-blame. However, on the whole, even as today's (elite, white, cis, straight) women proponents of the clean/ancestral lifestyle accept "full responsibility for creating a happy work-family balance, often through practices of personal well-being," [47] they fail to take into consideration the very different reality faced by most women and mothers in the United States. In this sense, the work of these bloggers can be seen as a form of neo-liberal feminism, or a form of feminism that suggests that women's advancement occurs via individual and market-based practices rather than through collective practices designed to bring about structural change.

Related to clean/ancestral eating and mommy blogging (think of this in terms of a Venn diagram) is neo-homesteading, a modern-day, largely individualist back-to-the-land movement. For instance, the Prairie

47   Mickey (2019), p. 108

Homestead blogger, Jill, who also hosts a podcast and sells mentorship services, a cookbook, "swag," and other homesteading supplies, states that she and her husband Christian did not grow up in the country. But, concerned they would become "robots" caught up in the "rat race," they bought sixty-seven acres of prairie land and a farm stand.

She continues, "However, this old-fashioned, unorthodox way of living didn't just stay in the barnyard for us . . . You see, once we realized we could think outside of the box and didn't have to float along with what modern culture told us we *should* be doing, we were hooked. What started with a passion for growing our own food eventually translated to Christian and I becoming serial entrepreneurs, living 100% debt-free, homeschooling our three children, and ultimately finding ourselves in the thick of creating a life we only could have dreamed of before. For our family and so many others, the modern homesteading movement is a way to slow down and create a healthier, more wholesome lifestyle" [emphasis in the original].

To be clear, homesteading[48] was quite literally part of the process by which European settlers took posses-

---

48 For more on homesteading, see National Archives (n.d.); on the ecological and health impacts thereof, check out Whyte (2016);

sion of Indigenous lands and often did so with financial and military support from the state. More pointedly, settler colonialism in North America involved the violent removal of Indigenous people from their lands. This, in turn, resulted in the forcible disruption of Indigenous food systems, with negative impacts on health. In the twentieth and twenty-first centuries, this violence continued via the impact of infrastructure projects, military and industrial pollution, and climate change on ecosystems. Contemporary homesteading should therefore not be seen as a form of "hip" self-sufficiency and a way to "opt out" of the system (as if that was possible), but rather as reflective of romanticized fantasies of settler occupation of unceded Indigenous land and the continuation of this violence.

Here, we must note two things. First, not all modern-day homesteaders give up their urban and suburban lives to move to the country. In fact, there's a whole urban homesteading movement wherein city-dwellers, many of whom are low-income and/or people of color, seek to gain a degree of self-sufficiency by starting collective farms and community gardens on abandoned lots, small individual gardens in their

and finally, on the relationship between immigration and settler colonialism, read Tuck & Yang (2012).

backyards, or even just on apartment terraces and windowsills. Second, regardless of whether or not we engage in neo-homesteading, all of us are settlers on unceded territory, unless we are Indigenous ourselves or our ancestors were forcibly brought here as enslaved people. For some decolonization activists and scholars, this even holds true of racialized immigrants to the United States whose own homelands may have been part of European colonial empires, though they acknowledge that this relationship to US settler colonialism differs from that of white European immigrants.

It's important to briefly return to those terms "clean" and "ancestral" often utilized by GFLC diet promoters. It's not just that these terms portray eating choices and practices, past and present, in oversimplified terms (though they certainly do that). And it's also not just that the foods associated with clean and ancestral eating are economically out of reach for a great many, though that's also true (there's a reason people mockingly call Whole Foods "Whole Paycheck"). It's that framing a diet as "clean" and/or "ancestral" traffics in "Happy Hunza"-esque racist and colonial tropes (think about how traditional foods from the Global South like chia seeds, goji berries, and quinoa are called "superfoods"), while simultaneously suggesting the foodways of communities of color are ultimately "dirty" and moreover, uncivilized. But these uncouth and dirty foodways can be recuperated—it would seem—by white people . . .

Consider the case of the (now infamous) white health coach and social media personality Arielle Haspel. In 2019, Haspel and her husband decided to open a "clean" Chinese restaurant in New York City. Motivated by the desire to offer patrons a locale where they could eat dishes like Lo Mein without feeling "icky" afterward, Haspel and her husband opened up "Lucky Lee's" (Haspel's husband's last name is Lee, though he is Jewish and not of Asian descent). Lucky Lee's was apparently decorated in bamboo and jade themes. The menu's font was chopstick-inspired. On that menu, Haspel offered a dish, which was presumably non-"icky," called "Hi-Lo Mein" (no really, that's what it was reportedly called).

Lucky Lee's didn't last long; however, underpinnings of racism and classism continue in the broader GFLC milieu. Sociologist Karen Wilkes argues that young, thin, elite, white, cis women are not only the leaders of clean/ancestral diet markets, but that wellness functions as an "emblem" of whiteness in this milieu. But clean/ancestral diet marketing *also* relies on the notion, in true

neoliberal form, that these diets are accessible to all—
requiring only the necessary work of self-management.
In this sense, the distinction inherent in clean/ancestral
eating and self-care markets more broadly is both held
up as morally and aesthetically aspirational and down-
played at the same time. More specifically, as Wilkes
explains, the elite white femininity that underpins
clean/ancestral markets simultaneously relies on claims
of both exceptionalism and universality. But while
white people continue to profit as leaders of these alternative food movements and markets, the exploitative,
low-status, low-wage, repetitive, and hazardous labor
that underpins all stages of food production—including
for those food products evangelized in clean/alternative
diets—is mostly undertaken by poor and working-class
people of color.

Harder, Better, Faster, Stronger

To be fair, white, cis men are also highly influential in
the clean/ancestral diet world and treat self-care and
self-improvement in an entrepreneurial manner, as well.
It's just that in these cases, lifestyle changes are framed
not as a way to achieve greater well-being on behalf of
oneself and one's family, but rather as a way to be—
as the song by the French electronic duo Daft Punk

goes—"harder, better, faster, stronger."[49] Blogs, social media, and books authored by men almost never reference changes made on behalf of the family. That work is left to women, apparently.

Consider the Primal Blueprint company, run by Mark Sisson—arguably a prominent individual in the paleo world. Sisson sells books, food products, supplements, courses and more (his Primal Kitchen products are commonly found at natural food stores, chains, and online sellers alike). In the "About" section of his website, Sisson too details his clean/ancestral self-care journey, except that his story centers around regaining the athletic endurance lost to over-exercising and suboptimal health. The linked YouTube video on the "About" page, "Live Awesome with the Primal Blueprint," features Sisson not only performing various feats of athleticism (apparently now possible thanks to his awesome blueprint, or the plan and products that you can purchase via his site) but also a man (presumably Sisson himself) cooking a steak and cutting up vegetables.

---

49   This line comes from Daft Punk's 2001 song (https://www.youtube.com/watch?v=yydNF8tuVmU&ab_channel=DaftPunk) as well as journalist Amanda Mull's excellent 2018 takedown of tech-bro clean/ancestral eating as a form of hidden dieting behavior.

What are the benefits of his blueprint? According to his website:

> We provide a complete diet, exercise and lifestyle philosophy, along with various products, services and community support, to help you enjoy effortless weight loss, vibrant health and boundless energy. The Primal Blueprint is based on lifestyle principles that have governed human health, evolution and peak performance for over two million years, and is supported by respected research in the fields of epigenetics and evolutionary biology.

Hearkening back to the Introduction to this book, notice here how Sisson's diet relies on notions of both "restoration" and "optimization."[50] Also take note of the ways in which his claims are based on the entanglement of personal embodied experience and references to scientific evidence.

Similar to Sisson are the "biohacking" men of the tech world, such as Dave Asprey, who parlayed his skillset into creating the nutrition and wellness company Bulletproof. In the "About" section of the Bulletproof website, Asprey's journey to optimization is described like this: it began with faltering energy during a Tibet trek through the mountains 18,000 feet above sea level.

50   See Derkatch (2018).

Handed a traditional butter tea, he suddenly felt rejuvenated, body and mind, and the "biohacker" in him was determined to find out why. Enter Bulletproof products. In other words, Asprey, a wealthy, North American, white, cis man apparently hacked and *improved upon* a traditional Tibetan drink. But unlike the fleeting success of Lucky Lee's, Bulletproof raised a total of $80 million in funding by 2020 and its products are now found throughout the United States.

According to the website: ". . . [Bulletproof offers the ability to] take control of your own biology, you're in the driver's seat. The world is your open road. Bulletproof is the high-octane gas that gets you where you want to go. Athlete? Check. Mathlete? Check. For the CEOs, the churners and the burners, the parents, the dreamers, the people who want to be the best version of themselves." It's true that "parents" are in the mix of those mentioned who would benefit from consuming Bulletproof's "high-octane" health and wellness products, such as coffee and collagen. Nevertheless, the overall frame is one of enhanced strength, agility, performance, and acuity. In other words, self-care for the men of the clean/ancestral eating world looks like enhancing individual power and dominance.

Interestingly, biohacking and other tech-bro forms of clean/ancestral eating (as well as intermittent fasting, something Twitter mogul Jack Dorsey is said to engage in) have been described by commentators as a way in which men can engage in dieting behavior—something traditionally associated with femininity—and yet do so in ways culturally associated with elite, (white) masculinity: that is, not counting calories, but "disrupting calories," in the words of the journalist Monica Hesse.

But could the engagement by men in this form of dieting behavior, however cool and hip it might seem to be, have something to do with larger structural anxieties? Journalist Thomas Stackpole, who has dabbled in intermittent fasting himself, seems to think so, and we agree: "Today's eating disorder is as likely to come in the guise of a diet that purports to optimize you to survive and thrive in late capitalism as it is one that claims to make you beach-body ready . . . In an era when so many of us feel the world spiraling out of control, maybe it's just the promise of being able to control something—to will a change, any change, into being—that's the draw."

In sum, the contemporary clean/ancestral eating and functional medicine movements, as with complementary and alternative medicine, more generally, have the effect of reinforcing not only key neoliberal ideals, but gender essentialism. Whereas men emphasize power, technology, and control, women, by contrast, highlight embodied experience, family, and care. Both, however, emphasize self-discovery, self-improvement, autonomous choice, personal responsibility, and market practices (both in terms of consumption and self-marketing) as a means by which to not only restore health but to advance or optimize it in an increasingly precarious world.

Recent Shifts in the Clean/Ancestral Eating Milieu

In September 2020 the Whole30 recently held a "Community Cares Summit"—a four-day, $79 series of virtual workshops. The webpage for the workshops begins with a quote from Audre Lorde about the importance of participating in shaping the future. Advertised workshops were said to revolve around key questions of "What now? What next? What are our most nurturing ways forward?" and covered such topics as "resistance visibility, politics of food and body, reimagining community, voting with resources, rest, recuperation, inter-industry accountability" and more. It was clear that the organizers of the summit took great pains to ensure the presenters represented diverse backgrounds. And many of the presenters referenced social justice work and/or scholarship in their bios. As well, a number of workshops over the course of the four days did cover social issues such as industry accountability and making

Whole30 work inclusive of individuals with disabilities and chronic illnesses.

Even more notable was that the summit kicked off with a reading of Audre Lorde's "Learning from the 60s" and featured one workshop on "Intention + Impact" and another entitled "Decolonizing the Kitchen." And while the description for the latter workshop only mentioned that audience members could "learn about culture in the kitchen," the bios for the panelists described such interests as food sovereignty and decolonization of food systems.

Even so, the majority of the workshops over the course of the summit focused on individual self-care practices (including cooking demonstrations, breathwork, herbalism, and physical activity classes) as well as sessions exclusively for Whole30 certified coaches on such topics as being "financially fit," dealing with difficult clients, expanding one's brand on social media, and confronting imposter syndrome so as to better earn one's worth.

Herein, the Whole30 summit exemplifies the "both/and" of current self-care markets. Whole30 appears to have taken a long hard look at the social impact of their business practices, and the changes they have made are commendable. For instance, Whole30 has increasingly featured content from individuals of color on Instagram (and other clean/ancestral eating promoters have taken similar or related actions). In doing so, they have leveraged the power and influence of their company to promote underrepresented health coaches, chefs, and other wellness professionals. This, in turn, not only has the potential to increase economic opportunities for said professionals but may help broaden the reach of needed forms of care to communities that have had less exposure and/or access.

What's more, after the murder of George Floyd, Whole30 co-founder Melissa Urban took an active and unapologetic role in shutting down criticisms of the company's support of Black Lives Matter protests on the company's social media accounts. Whole30 has also explicitly supported LGBTQIA+ rights by both posting on social media in support of these communities and featuring content from out LGBTQIA+ individuals. Other high-profile GFLC promoters have done the same.

Considering that taking these actions may have negatively impacted Whole30's bottom line (which, while successful, is still a fairly small self-care and wellness company compared to a behemoth like Goop), it was a bold stance, indeed. But did it go far enough?

The Illusion of Change

In some ways, contemporary clean/ancestral eating and functional medicine might be seen as examples of what sociologist Phil Brown and coauthors call "Embodied

Health Movements" (EHS), or movements that seek to address ill health by challenging medical-scientific assertions about the causes of and remedies for given conditions. In such movements, lay individuals draw upon embodied experience as a form of health knowledge. Further, these movements "blur the boundaries between lay and expert forms of knowledge," often including collaborations between trained professionals and illness sufferers.

But, by and large, today's food-based health movements do not offer a critique of the ways that broader social conditions and inequalities shape health and illness outcomes. They are reformist endeavors rather than revolutionary ones.

To be more specific, the growth in the ancient/clean eating milieu may be a response to disenchantment with mainstream institutions that shape health outcomes. Clean/ancestral diets and functional medicine practices are surely, for the majority of their followers, attempts to address very real embodied pain and suffering. In this sense, feeling like one is taking control of the situation by making lifestyle choices may feel like a salve or a project, like motion or empowerment.

More broadly, food-based self-care movements may reflect a reaction to the precarity of life under neoliberalism (as tends to be the case with contemporary self-care movements, in general).

But rather than pointing to the need for collective organizing for radical change, they suggest that autonomous, entrepreneurial self-discovery, self-care, and self-optimization by individuals constitute the key to change and control. Thus, they can end up obscuring the stark realities of neoliberal and neocolonial capitalist inequality and its cultural, legislative, political, and economic drivers even if they use their platforms to highlight contemporary injustices in some of their messaging.

The fact that so many of these food-based health movements appear to be driven by women does not change this fact. And it does nothing to truly advance gender equality, in that many clean/ancestral personalities effectively reaffirm essentialist notions that women are primarily responsible for the health and care practices in the family, while ignoring the larger structural constraints on the choices that other women and mothers are able to make.

Given the ongoing nature of gender inequality (an inequality that is, of course, always crosscut by other forms of oppression and marginalization) and given the neoliberal expectations for health and self-optimization, the fact that clean/ancestral self-care blogs, social media, and books frame the causes and solutions to ill-health in this manner and reaffirm essentialist notions of gender is, sadly, not surprising. That doesn't mean things shouldn't be otherwise.

Yes, there are always exceptions. Yes, these lifestyle changes do offer some *individuals* useful tools to improve health and quality of life.

But what effects[51] does the increased consumption of natural, organic, grass-fed/pastured/wild, GFLC foods by the affluent individuals who can afford them have on the food apartheid and health disparities faced by many low-income and marginalized communities? What does the clean/ancestral diet industry have to say about the fact that, perhaps as a result of declining sales in the Global North, "Big Food" has pushed aggressively into the Global South, changing local diets in the process?[52] What impact do these diets have on the occu-

---

51   To learn more about the exploitation and extraction discussed in this section, see: Brones (2018); Fair Trade Certified (n.d.); Freudenberg (2014); Karavolias (2019); Ochoa Ayala (2020); Sainato (2019); and Stuckler & Nestle (2012).

52   Stuckler & Nestle (2012) note that the processed food industries pushed into Global South markets not only through mass-marketing campaigns and foreign investments, but also through the takeover of domestic food companies. Though trade

pational health and safety conditions for farm workers or for employees at Whole Foods?

The answer to all of the above is: nothing (of any substance). Worse still, the increased desire and extractive demand for clean/ancestral diet foods such as avocados and coconuts in the Global North has been linked to ecological damage and ongoing exploitative labor in the Global South. And in this sense, the Global North's whims for the foodstuffs of the Global South can be seen as another form of colonialism.

Whether in their subtle or explicit forms, and regardless of the intentions of their purveyors, contemporary (elite) food trends cannot be divorced from a long history in which Europeans have profited off the culinary traditions, expertise, land, and labor of Black and Brown bodies. This is not to say that white people shouldn't eat foods that bring pleasure and nourishment if those foods don't originally hail from the parts of Europe from which their ancestors hail. But it does mean that their (our) food politics cannot be limited to their (our) own self-enhancement and self-advancement.

plays a part, the major reason why diets in the Global South transitioned from a basis in traditional foods to highly processed food products has to do with the actions of global producers headquartered in the Global North.

Undoubtedly, modifications to our own lifestyles or even existing systems are easier to grasp conceptually and to enact materially than dismantling and replacing them with something truly different. We get that. And we certainly don't have an easy, breezy, ten-point plan for enacting radical change (and frankly, if two relatively privileged white people offer you such a plan, you should probably run). With that said, the path to self-care, health, and wellness should neither obscure nor augment exploitation and injustice.

In the final chapter of this book, we lay out different care-based movements that we draw inspiration from, and which illustrate that collective care can help address the crises we all find ourselves caught up in (though we are caught up in very different ways depending on who we are). But first, we close out this chapter by contrasting the aforementioned authors and bloggers with another set that calls for a decolonizing approach.

Decolonize!

So, how can we decolonize our approach to food as a means of self-care and wellness? We felt that it made sense to look to a cookbook as a counterpoint. Specifically, we turned to Luz Calvo and Catrióna Rueda Esquibel's

Decolonize Your Diet: Plant-based Mexican-American Recipes for Health and Healing.

Let's start with the same questions we've been asking, for example: How do the authors frame the causes of illness? These authors flatly reject the notion that individual lifestyle factors are *the cause* of illness or the pathway to health. Rather, they point to the "single-minded corporate worldview" that values profit over the health of the earth. They examine how the interface of policy and industry has helped create tremendous profits in the food sector but harmed the health of the public. Calvo and Rueda Esquibel describe, at the international level, past trade deals such as the North American Free Trade Agreement (NAFTA), which had a devastating impact on Mexican farmers, particularly indigenous farmers. They further discuss the impact that international relations, policies, and agreements have had on immigration patterns and the subsequent effect on diet and health for immigrant communities. Thus, even when they do reference lifestyle factors such as diet, they situate those micro-level factors in a larger structural context.

In a nutshell: for these authors, the root cause of ill health in the United States is five hundred years of colonialism.

What benefits do Calvo and Rueda Esquibel attribute to the way of eating outlined in their cookbook? The authors do offer particular recipes and suggest particular ingredients—it is, after all, a cookbook. Yet they underline that there are no hard-and-fast rules: "In a decolonial framework, there is room for multiple ways of eating, so we don't believe that everyone needs to make the same food choices." They point to the fact that even attempting to introduce more traditional foods into one's diet is a fraught process, given the industrial, corporate food supply chain and production system. Thus, they view their recipes as "living documents" that the reader can adjust as needed based on what is on hand or available.

Further, they point to the diversity in and evolution of cultural modes of eating. In this sense, they are neither seeking to promote nor romanticize some "universal" or "primal" form of eating that is best suited to human physiology. Highlighting the communal nature of food and cooking and the collective nature of sharing meals, they suggest that the key ingredient to any dish is *love*.

Unlike clean/ancestral diet and functional medicine authors, Calvo and Rueda Esquibel address issues of inequality and position themselves within complex systems of power. They identify themselves as queer Chicanas/os of mixed backgrounds living in the United States. They repeatedly acknowledge and honor First Nation individuals and communities, upon whose knowledge they draw. They honor the earth, plants, and animals that provide sustenance for humans.

Calvo and Rueda Esquibel also express gratitude for the workers who produce the food we eat (highlighting the exploitation they face). Finally, they point to the fact that gendered labor within the household, including that related to food, has often been unacknowledged and moreover coercive: "We believe that any cookbook and discussion of food preparation that doesn't address the gendered conditions of labor may be seen to reinforce oppressive relations. We are not calling for a return of Chicanas and Central American women to the kitchen. *We are calling for the liberation of the kitchen*" (emphasis added).

A separate 2016 article by Esquibel on decolonizing one's diet concludes with a quote by Sariwa Fresh of the Oakland People's Kitchen Collective:

> The meal is a political act. We cook to intervene in systems of white supremacy and capitalism. There are recipes of resilience, passed from generation to generation, and surviving migration, enslavement, and displacement. This is not farm-to-table. This meal is farm-to-the-kitchen-to-the-table-to-the-streets. We are here to feed rebellions and nourish revolutions. This meal is a culinary intervention to decolonize foodways.

Decolonizing diet (and by extension health) is thus not about eating certain foods and avoiding others (though of course industrial food production does cause substantial harm to the bodies of both eaters and laborers, which is likely why the People's Kitchen Collective uses local ingredients whenever possible in preparing community meals). Rather, the focus is on the web of connections between people, the land, animals, health, and social justice. More specifically, as the Indigenous scholar-activist Kyle Whyte puts it, the emphasis is placed on examining how the relations between ". . . food production, labor, preparation, consumption, and disposal are woven tightly with land tenure, a community's way of life, reciprocal gift giving and life sustenance, connecting people in a community, and respect."

The solution is therefore not one of individual acts or niche food and health markets, nor self-marketing opportunities. The solution is collective action and a radical rethinking of larger systems of social organization, politics, economy, and land. As the People's Kitchen Collective puts it, recipes help dismantle white supremacy, and meals fill the belly and nourish souls, feed minds, and fuel movements. And the only rules at the table are "justice, equity, and freedom."

Chapter 4

MORE *CARE*, LESS *SELF*?
HOW TO (HOPEFULLY) MOVE
BEYOND COMPLAINT, CRITIQUE,
AND COLONIALITY

When the Antidote Is Just More of the Same Poison

Let's bring it back to where we began, with Gwyneth Paltrow of Goop, aka "GP," influencer extraordinaire. On May 28, 2020, three days after Black Minneapolis resident George Floyd was brutally murdered by police, GP posted a characteristic black square with white type in the traditional Goop-y font on the Goop Instagram account.

But this time, the message was different. It was not a photo of racially diverse pregnant women, posed next to each other in a beautiful rainbow as a plug for Goop's prenatal vitamins and "pre-pregnancy belly oil" (yes, we are describing an actual post), nor were these photos of delicious looking salads or chic furniture or stills from dream vacations of pre-pandemic times past. The May 28, 2020 post asked: "What part do I play? #JusticeForGeorgeFloyd." With this, GP reiterated questions posed by Robin DiAngelo (author of *White Fragility*), emphasized her support for the Black Lives Matter protests, proclaimed that white people must do the work of undoing racial inequality, and even provided links to organizations that members of the Goop community might consider donating to, including: the NAACP, the Equal Justice Initiative, Color of Change, the Southern Poverty Law Center, and the Minnesota Freedom Fund.

At the time of this writing, the post received 4,478 likes and over one hundred comments,[53] ranging from "Thank you for this call to action!" to "This is what we want to see from Goop!" to "Pay Black creators!" to ". . . read books from Black authors about race! [instead of DiAngelo]" to "Hey @goop is there a page where we can see how much you've donated to these places??" to "Well your Instagram has been very fuckin whitewashed until recently when this movement started . . . start with that and ask why there aren't any POC especially Black people on your posts before you [just recently] joined the BLM movement." And finally, at least one commenter stated that she'll "★sigh★" be forced to unfollow Goop, apparently based on what we can only assume are Goop's new "biased"—that is, liberal—politics and polemics (this particular poster describes herself in her bio as a "Free Thinker" and an "American"—in addition to a "Worker Bee," "Mama," and "Wife," of course).

---

53 It should be noted, however, that Instagram posts featuring GP herself, for instance wearing a cute cardigan, often receive upwards of 40K likes and many more than 100 comments.

The most recent comment simply said "Garbage" (with a wastebasket emoji).

Since the spring of 2020, Goop has posted several more times about racial justice, proclaiming #black-livesmatter, #justiceforbreonna, and #sayhername. And many more Black and Brown faces have appeared on Goop's Instagram feed: Race scholar Ibram X. Kendi was featured on the Goop podcast over the summer, and, at one point, Goop's Insta feed even featured a post raising the question "What does defund the police mean?" (Notably, this one got a lot of negative comments and a ton of unfollows . . .)

So how do we reconcile #sayhername on the Goop Insta with the simultaneous promotion of $4,500 tickets to wellness retreats featuring sound therapy, sensory deprivation tech, and access to the newest detox regimens? It's seems very possible that Goop's newfound wokeness is all just a marketing ploy (this is what we suspect). It's also *possible* that GP and the executives at Goop are earnestly asking themselves how they can leverage the power of a corporation valued at more than $250 million to make real change (we doubt it).[54]

54   It is also worth mentioning here that Gwyneth Paltrow came under fire in Spring 2021 for a blog post on the Goop website: https://goop.com/wellness/detox/gwyneth-paltrows-long

This shift in rhetoric is not exclusive to Goop, but rather is seen across the self-care industry or self-care industrial complex as a whole, and even beyond within everyday conversations. Self-care marketers increasingly utilize the language of social and racial justice, as well as feminism, and point to our collective responsibility to make change. At the same time, self-care continues to be a highly lucrative industry wherein wealthy, white, cis women are, by and large, both the marketers and the market. The industry continues to rely on nostalgia, inspiration, and *as*piration, as well as themes that appropriate "The East" and Indigeneity in marketing materials—and these populations typically do not benefit from the sale of self-care and wellness products, even when these products have legitimate origins in the Global South and Indigenous cultures and locales. The self-care movement as a whole continues to promote the idea that the achievement of health and wellness comes from individual (market-based) choices rather than structural and collective change.

-term-detox-tips/. In this post, she describes how she had COVID-19 early on in the pandemic, and now suffers from symptoms of Long Covid. She goes on to explain how she is making a full recovery via an "intuitive fasting" diet, and uses the post as an opportunity to sell Goop products that she says will help others recover from Long Covid symptoms, including vitamin supplements, a detoxifying "super powder," a hyaluronic skin serum, and an infrared sauna blanket (which goes for $500).

These contradictions are indicators of the strange self-care moment we are living, in which on-the-ground social movements have fought hard to force radical ideas into mainstream conversations, while, at the same time, those mainstream conversations rarely consider the radical roots of real social justice activism or political organizing (nor do they acknowledge what would actually be required to change anything—and why would they? That would be bad for business!). The rhetoric remains superficial and individualistic, and ultimately maintains the deepest structural inequality—but wraps it up in pretty DEI packaging.

As a reminder, in this version of self-care, the maxim "the personal is political" is a renewed rallying cry (*and* has been fully recuperated by the capitalist marketplace) and "allyship" and "intersectionality" are of serious concern (*and* good for business). Oh, the contradictions . . .

To be sure, offering people products, goods, services, and tips to cope with life's hardships is important and useful. People are suffering *now*. As scholar-activists Edwin Mayorga, Lekey Leidecker, and Daniel Orr de Gutierrez argue in a 2019 article on decolonizing higher education, "in order to build a future outside of this reality, we must first survive it." No one, particularly those from marginalized and multiply marginalized backgrounds, should sacrifice their health and well-being in the service of a larger political goal (especially since ensuring our health and well-being *is* a political goal).

We all need care, whether in the form of nutritious food, rest, sleep, and sometimes even mindfulness. And the pursuit of these things might be individualized, may not tackle the structural problems at stake, but sometimes we still just need *something*, as it feels so hard to find alternatives for taking care of ourselves with the current state of the world being what it is. This is where *self*-care tends to enter the conversation—and it makes sense that it does.

We would do well to remember: alternative, DIY, functional, and other forms of "holistic" self-care medicine have always been used by people who have historically been prevented from access to reliable or affordable allopathic medicine, or who have been framed as patients "not worth believing" by traditional medical professionals. Often, these patients are women of color. For instance, racialized and gendered discrepancies in pain management, particularly, are well documented: doctors are less likely to believe women and folks of color about the level of pain they are experiencing. The same is likely true of chronic illnesses, including those illnesses that are difficult to diagnose. Given the substantial health disparities faced by women around the world (and within the US health care system), particularly women of color and those who are poor, disabled, migrants, Indigenous, and/or trans or non-binary, it is imperative to remember the myriad reasons why individuals take up self-care practices to begin with.

But: unlike the radical wellness projects that have understood self-care in a more truly and deeply community-oriented, justice-seeking way—projects which emerged squarely out of working class, Black, Brown, Indigenous, immigrant, disabled, and queer and trans communities—the "softer," "gentler," neoliberal version found in today's self-care moment relies on strategies that are ultimately compatible and assimilable with the existing order. In this sense, they too often mask the roots of the ill health, burnout, trauma, and disillusionment that we experience because of interlocking systems of ableism, colonialism, and neoliberal racial capitalism in the first place. As Audre Lorde stated more than forty years ago: "The master's tools will never dismantle the master's house. They may allow us temporarily to beat him at his own game, but they will never enable us to bring about genuine change."[55]

On this point, we can't forget that the responsibility for care is not only individualized, it is structurally offloaded by the state and shifted on to the public.

55   Lorde (1984 [1979]), p. 112.

During the hellscape that was the year 2020, there was an outpouring of financial support made via the social-fundraising platform GoFundMe. More than $625 million was raised for COVID-19 relief alone. These funds, often offered by average Americans who reached deep into their own pockets in order to help out, certainly eased a degree of suffering for those contending most directly with the health and economic hardships wrought by the pandemic. But social-media-based fundraising platforms can be no substitute for robust social safety net programs, universal health care, and other policies that reduce income and wealth inequality. And they are certainly no substitute for timely, adequate, and durable government economic stimulus packages—or a living wage.

How to address the tension between short-term needs and long-term goals is an age-old dilemma (and the source of much consternation and debate) within social justice organizing and movement work. There are no easy answers.

Bearing this in mind: how can we all take better care of ourselves and each other in the here and now, with an eye toward destroying the systems that continue to oppress so many of us? How can we care—including for ourselves—while acknowledging *self*-care's limitations within today's alternative health and wellness industry (and alongside a state that shirks responsibility for even a modicum of support)? It is at this nexus, between this desperate need and its commodification (a commodification which makes it inaccessible for too many), that we must fight for care, and *use care to fight*. And it feels like now, the stakes have never been higher.

Care Against Colonialism

Thanks to the work of so many BIPOC activists, scholars, and scholar-activists, we know that decolonization is as much about the process as it is about the endpoint. In her 2013 book *Undoing Border Imperialism*, South Asian Canadian activist, writer, and educator Harsha Walia describes decolonization as a "generative and prefigurative process whereby we create the conditions in which we want to live and the social relations we want to have—for ourselves *and* everyone else" while simultaneously organizing against "authoritarian governance, oppressive hierarchies, and capitalist economies." Because we are all positioned within existing systems of power differently, the work of decolonization calls upon us to "learn about and challenge each other in our complicities and contradictions within asymmetric relations of power and oppression, as we unlearn colonial strategies that foster competition and division among each other."[56]

Decolonization is thus a praxis that is relational, lived, and which involves resisting the existing order while simultaneously working to build something new. In this formulation, "*self*-care" creates a conundrum, a paradox, or maybe even an oxymoron—as a decolonial version of care must not be individualistic, but instead collectivist (i.e., more *care*, less *self*).

In this vein, here are some movements that we are inspired by around the world:

Women fight together for autonomy in movements across Africa, South Asia, and South America—for example, the Gulabi Gang or Pink Saris who strike back against rapists and the women farmers of India who engage in eco-socialist land protection and community care via subsistence practices. Under the restrictions of an oppressive government, people have also been pro-actively and aggressively fighting for uterine autonomy, reproductive control, and gender justice in Mexico, Chile, and Argentina for some time now—in addition to in Poland and other places around the world (we hope that more organizers in the US will take cues from these powerful movements, particularly in light of the brutal

56   Walia (2013), p. 107-108.

restrictions on abortion, care for trans kids, and related forms of health care in the United States since the overturning of *Roe v. Wade*).

Other international movements that do not center women, specifically, but which are often led by cis and trans women and gender-diverse individuals, and which emphasize autonomy, determination, struggles around labor (including reproductive labor), and community care in the face of neoliberal austerity include: the Zapatistas of Chiapas Mexico (an independence and justice movement comprised of Indigenous people in southern Mexico that has been fighting neoliberalism for more than thirty years), the Argentinian horizontalist movements (which have advocated for a decentralized, federated form of social organization from the early-aughts through today), and the ongoing struggles of the anarchist/autonomist movements in present-day Rojava (a self-declared autonomous region near northeastern Syria which promotes gender equality and radical egalitarianism, more broadly).

Back in the US, the ecological care framework put forward by the Indigenous water protectors of Standing Rock around the Dakota Access Pipeline[57] is an impor-

---

57 The water protectors framing their work as *care* is also discussed by Hobart & Kneese (2020).

tant example of a form of radical community care, as is the work of activists with the Wet'suwet'en Nation who have come out against the Coastal GasLink pipeline in what Canadian settlers today call British Columbia. And the Movement for Black Lives[58] and related anti-racist and anti-fascist organizing, movement building, and direct action—including in the form of autonomous zones in Seattle and Portland (with all of the problems that came along with these)—re-center radical and communal care and draw attention to state neglect, oppression, and violence.

The disability justice and associated healing justice movement is another place where DIY care work—as a fully and always political practice—has been happening for decades. Disability justice activist, writer, and poet Leah Lakshmi Piepzna-Samarasinha describes the movement as a framework that centers the lives, needs, and organizing strategies of disabled queer and trans and Black and Brown people marginalized from mainstream disability rights organizing's white-dominated, single-issue focus.

---

58   https://m4bl.org/—It is imperative to remember that M4BL was a movement begun by three queer Black women.

In her 2018 book *Care Work: Dreaming Disability Justice*, Piepzna-Samarasinha chronicles her time with the Disability Justice Collective (DJC—with roots in Toronto and Detroit) in the early 2000s, linking that work to the earlier history of care work as it was enacted by radical, communist, racial justice organizers associated with the Black Panthers, and to Indigenous healing practitioners across communities and groups. Her discussion of "care webs"—networks wherein disabled folks work together to figure out how to support each other, practically, on the ground, and every day—brings home how care cannot ever actually be "*self*-care" for disabled people. It is always a process that must be configured, executed, and worked upon by many people, together, in community. However, within all of these movements, caring for the self is, in fact, still understood as imperative—it's just that oppressed folks have always known that "it takes a village," and that when no one else has your back, you have to take care of yourself (and your friends). Here, reproducing one's self is part and parcel of reproducing entire marginalized communities.

If we take seriously the notion that this type of reproductive work has historically been feminized but *not* undertaken primarily by elite, white, cis women, we can begin to see how care—including "self-care"—might be decolonized. Consider, for instance, the role of Black and Latina trans women such as Marsha P. Johnson and Sylvia Rivera in the Stonewall Uprising and associated radical queer political organizing. It was not white women—nor gay white men—who were at the helm, and instead this foundational political (and often unrewarded and invisibilized) caring organizing work was done largely by trans women of color, including sex workers. This is just one more example of how self-care has been taken up by feminized, racialized, queer, poor, immigrant, and disabled folks—because who else was going to do it?

Of course, individuals feeling good is important (the revolution should be pleasurable—as Emma Goldman, Adrienne Maree Brown, and many others remind us)! But the DJC's way of thinking about care webs and reproducing marginalized communities while feeling good stands in contradistinction to the notion that you should care for others primarily because it will make you feel good about yourself (today's neoliberal motto). Instead, care in these DIY disability justice communities meaningfully centers *everyone's* survival—while simultaneously honoring internal differences in terms of needs within the group. Protocols for care here do not always go smoothly: considering the actual operation of care webs brings home how much the experience and reality of disability—and the emotional and physical work that is required to care for those in need in various justice-focused communities—has historically fallen on the backs of Black, Brown, and Indigenous women, disproportionately. But the point is that folks in these communities have consistently strived toward accountability, care, *and pleasure*, even within asymmetrical relations of power.

In a 2020 article, radical scholar and organizer Dean Spade similarly centers the importance of mutual aid in caring for each other better, looking to the work of Mutual Aid Disaster Relief (MADR), a network that provides mutual aid for marginalized folks in times of structural and ecological disaster. Spade also points out that the serious care work of mutual aid is regularly diminished, and often precisely because it is feminized. Such work is nevertheless vital to supporting survival while building toward new forms of *self-determination* and *self-organization* (and the "self-" in these terms means much more than just one individual; they instead invoke the determination and organization of entire communities).

Collective care and mutual aid aren't perfect processes: they are messy and often characterized by conflict and competing needs. Nevertheless, the care described by Piepzna-Samarasinha, Spade, and other radical organizers and activists suggests the two-fold work of dismantling the systems that currently exist while simultaneously building something new in their wake. This is what Rupa Marya, a medical doctor writing about decolonizing health care, describes as the dual work of decolonization: dismantlement and reintegration. Marya states, "We must reintegrate what has been divided and conquered in our societies, between our peoples, between us and the natural world around us, and within ourselves . . . We must dismantle those systems of domination that create and recreate cycles of trauma and inflammation, those systems that work in the service of capitalism."

These powerful examples remind us of how we might care for each other now and in the future, and what is at stake.

So, what else can any of us actually do to *decolonize* self-care? Before we can answer this, it is necessary to consider that "self-care" as a concept has possibly reached the nadir of its contradiction (and we hope it is clear by now that it *is* a contradiction).

Are we in a time and a place where the part about the "self" has fully eclipsed the part about the "care"?

Are we in a time and a place where *care*—if we conceive of it as at least partially oriented outward, implying a bond of sorts, and perhaps even calling up others who must be considered in relations of care—is no longer the primary term?

In today's popular framing, care (who needs it, who deserves it) has also been portrayed very differently for different people: Who tends to be positioned as the proper subject of self-care? Who is understood to deserve to take time off to recharge, to unwind, to re-create an identity? Who can afford to do so? How do deserving and affording here become mutually constitutive and indistinguishable? Are you—we—they—"worth it"? Do *you* deserve to "treat" yourself? With these questions raised, maybe we can consider that real justice right now might look like some folks having more access than others to "indulge" in self-care . . .

We are thinking here, for instance, of the protest actions of the "Wall of Moms" in Portland, Oregon during the summer of 2020. In much of the media framing, the moms who came out for racial justice, to support the Black Lives Matter protests, and to decry the murders of George Floyd and Breonna Taylor, appeared to be white cis women.

But racial justice activists quickly pointed out that Black mothers have been engaging in anti-racist activism forever, *because they had to be*—in order to protect their children. And there were further internal divisions within the Wall of Moms—were the white mom activists taking up too much space? Should they be putting their bodies on the line *more*? If they did so, though, was this really just a way for them to take the spotlight away from Black moms and other Black BLM organizers? Many were accused of doing just this, and ultimately, some people became very defensive.

And some of these defensive white women *were* clearly ill-intentioned, as, even though the whole point of their group was to protect Black protestors, they left Black women at the marches and demonstrations vulnerable and unprotected by putting themselves first (in what was a perhaps shameless and narcissistic act of *self*-care). In August 2020, the Wall of Moms group disintegrated, and many defected and joined a new, Black woman-led group, Mothers United for Black Lives.

What does this story tell us about decolonizing self-care? One takeaway is that people's intentions are not monolithic. Surely all of the moms came out for different reasons, and they had varying levels of commitment to racial justice (and personal stakes in this regard). What kinds of care were they each invested in? Self-care? Community care? Community care to benefit the self?? We will never know all of the different paths that brought folks out; but we can certainly ask for more from (or maybe even call out—or *in*) those that prioritized themselves and their own indulgences, those who privileged their own self-care over caring for others. And we can hold them accountable for their mistakes, learn from their mistakes, work on the process, and do a better job of caring in the future.

What You Can Do Today to Salvage Self-Care from our Capitalist and Colonialist Overlords

We are deeply inspired by the powerful movements that bring together dismantlement and reintegration, and we hope you are, too. But what about the folks who are not already involved? If we are in a moment in which there is too much *self* and too little *care*, how can we help change this and invert the equation?

Before we get into some specifics, let's first recognize that turning inward (or outward) has different stakes and resonances for different people. For some, given their own histories of privilege, turning inward, *self*-caring, seems narcissistic. For others, who have been oppressed and marginalized, it may feel more like justice. We would argue that simply remembering this difference— these asymmetries—is an important place to begin. We would all do well to remember that care—including *self*-care—has never been as accessible to some as it has been for others.

We are here to acknowledge the complexity of community care, self-care, and social justice, and to honor how imperfect *decolonizing* any of these things will invariably be under existing systems of power (that is: under an irresponsible and unaccountable neoliberal racial capitalist nation-state and global world order). And one thing we *don't* want is for overthinking and fear of critique to stymy action IRL.

The eternal struggle of political organizing and education is that this this work is always fraught, and that every action exists within multiply layered contexts and histories. Parsing out whether someone is truly "contributing to the movement" or just "taking up space" rarely has a conclusive answer. But that doesn't mean people shouldn't get out there and try to do something anyway. As we have tried to make clear, there is no outside of any of this, and no place of purity.

With all of that said, here are some things we try to keep in mind, based on the decolonial, revolutionary, and abolitionist writings and teachings that we have been fortunate enough to come in to contact with over the years—primarily from BIPOC scholars and activists.

First and foremost: In whatever way we move forward, it must be collective. And it must be led by Black and Indigenous people of color and those who are the most disenfranchised, those who have had the least access to care, and those who need it the most. So, listen to the words of folks in the most marginalized and vulnerable positions! This means listening to individuals and deferring to folks who have been more affected by structures of inequality than you have. If you are white people like we are, it means keeping quiet more often in movement spaces, and alternately speaking up about inequality when you are around other white people.

Secondly: If you are a white person and you profit from selling self-care-oriented goods and/or services, you might ask yourself how you can ensure that your work supports justice and not just your own economic advancement. For instance, you might offer your goods or services for free or for a nominal fee to BIPOC and individuals from other communities directly under siege from neoliberal racial capitalism.

And, finally: Remember that none of us can do everything, but all of us can make more ethical and politically attuned choices, and then do something with those choices. We all need to care for ourselves (and yes, this period of time right now is really damn stressful), but we can do this in ways that allows others to care for themselves, too (while also caring for each other!). And we can think of the bigger picture. And we can be less defensive. So maybe this last idea should actually come first—develop and refine your political compass (if you haven't already) and figure out how and where it makes sense (and where you have the capacity) to put your energy. Then, do it.

Ok, so you want more specifics?

This is tough, because we are also learning how to best support decolonial, anti-capitalist, anti-fascist, racial justice movements on the ground, ourselves, every day. But here you go—these are some of the ideas that we have come across in our lives that resonate with us, that we have learned from other people (and are continuing to learn). Maybe they will resonate with you, as well:

- Remember the notion that healing those parts of ourselves that are unwell and/or traumatized is important not just in its own right but so that we have the reserves to continue to fight for justice (not so that we can be more economically productive at our jobs and/or better self-entrepreneurs). So, of course, take care of yourself! It's unsustainable (and, frankly, ableist) to expect that political activism and organizing require operating at maximum speed, all the time. Seek care when you need it and give yourself time and space to rest and heal. This is especially important for those facing multiple forms of oppression. When society does not value you and your well-being, caring for yourself—as Audre Lorde argued—*is* a radical act.

• Improve your social well-being by connecting with, caring for, and reaching out to others. There is substantial evidence that forging and maintaining social connections is good for the health of all of us, of our communities. Conversely, alienation and loneliness are just not good for any of us, particularly during periods of crisis. By sharing resources and being there for one another—particularly through hard times—we can help one another get by in this toxic world and, at the same time, build community care and capacity (and this is very different from the neoliberal idea of caring for others because it makes you feel better about yourself).

• Focus on self-*enrichment*, not self-*optimization*. Read a book and learn about abolition, decolonization, revolution, and radical healing justice movements, alongside other people. And remember, we are each—in our own unique ways and from our own intersectional vantage points—unlearning the toxic societal messages that we've absorbed all our lives. Be gentle with yourself in unlearning those messages but also accountable for any harm you may cause to others, even if it's inadvertent. We all have work to do. We all make mistakes. What matters is how we respond to those mistakes.

- Get involved with collectives that offer everyday care in a real, community-oriented, justice-seeking style. For us in NYC, that means places like Heal Haus (offering yoga, meditation, and body and energy work), the Brooklyn Zen Center (featuring a BIPOC sangha), and the (now-defunct) Third Root Collective (which offered yoga, acupuncture, massage, community workshops, and so much more). Whether you go to these places for your own care or not (and we absolutely suggest that you do), if you have the means to, you can also donate money to them to help them keep their doors open and provide services to the folks who need it the most. Heal Haus, for instance, has a therapy fund that BIPOC folks can apply for. Beneficiaries receive eight sessions with a local therapist, as part of an initiative to support the mental health and well-being of people of color, who disproportionately face so many traumas and forms of structural, everyday violence. Similarly, the Third Root Collective solicited donations for their "collective care fund" to provide low- to no-cost care "where it's needed most—to Black, Indigenous People of Color, prioritizing local Flatbush residents, trans women and femmes, and disabled and formerly incarcerated community members" (https://thirdroot.org/our-mission/). Of course, none of these organizations are perfect—but, from what we know, they do emphasize internal accountability within the collectives themselves, in addition to external accountability to the surrounding communities and neighborhoods, which seems like a pretty solid step in the right direction when it comes to offering real communal care.

• Get involved with local Black-, Indigenous-, and other POC-led movements, collectives, and organizations. Many of the neighborhoods where we live have mutual aid groups, community fridges and gardens, and other collectives, some that formed during the COVID-19 pandemic—for instance Bed-Stuy Strong (BSS), led by young women of color in Bedford-Stuyvesant Brooklyn. BSS began as a way to raise funds and labor to buy and deliver groceries (and window air conditioner units in the hot summer months) to people in the neighborhood who couldn't afford to buy food (or ACs) or were unable to leave their houses. Also started in the midst of the pandemic and in light of escalating anti-Asian racism and xenophobia, "Heart of Dinner" is an NYC-based collective of individuals that delivers home-cooked meals to low-income Asian-American elders who couldn't leave their homes (the meals come complete with handwritten notes). Just remember, if you're a white person, you should not expect to be immediately welcomed into these movements, collectives, and organizations! But you can still support the work by helping spread their messages to others who need to hear them, by building relationships and coalitions, by donating to these groups if you can, and/or by offering your own time, labor, and services when and how they are needed.

- Train to be a medic, legal observer, court aid, food/water/support provider, or do other on-the-ground work for anti-capitalist racial justice movements' protests and other actions (or simply spread the word and offer money if and when you can). Support their strategies in the long-term, as well—a good place to start is by contacting local groups to find out what they need.

- Another option, of course, is to draw on networks you are already a part of, and/or get together with folks—like friends, neighbors, and family—and *create* care webs and collectives in order to provide each other with (different types of) needed support. Sharing and bartering food, goods, skills, and services (including things like massages, help with cleaning, etc.) makes care provision and access sustainable—and pleasurable.

- And, finally, protest injustice in your town or city or on your campus (following the lead of local organizers who are most affected by the issues at hand) in whatever way you can. Remember, not everyone has the ability to engage in street-level protests or direct action and not all of us face the same risks from police when we do. But: we can all come together and ORGANIZE.

There is really no shortage of ways to get involved with existing care communities. And while we mention NYC-based organizations here, there are groups and collectives all over the country doing this work, including the Kindred Southern Healing Justice Collective, the Black Emotional and Mental Health Collective (BEAM), the Disability Justice Collective (all of these groups are now national), and the Bad Ass Visionary Healers (in the Bay Area and beyond). These are just some of the most well-known groups, too—if you do some research, we guarantee you'll find people doing this care work where you live.

★ ★ ★

As always, Audre Lorde's words remain relevant and powerful: "One of the hardest things to accept is learning to live within uncertainty and neither deny it nor hide behind it. Most of all, to listen to the messages of uncertainty without allowing them to immobilize me, nor keep me from the certainties of those truths in which I believe. I turn away from any need to justify the future—to live in what has not yet been. Believing, working for what has not yet been while living fully in the present now."[59]

59   Lorde (1988), p. 131.

The first step toward healing from the harms and traumas of colonization, colonialism, and coloniality is believing that another way forward is possible. The next step is collective action—walking the walk (and the talk) together. The work of real change will be characterized by fears of the unknown. It will be uncomfortable. Working across difference will inevitably involve conflict and incommensurability. But, as decolonial scholars Eve Tuck & K. Wayne Yang have said, "we will find out the answers as we get there."[60]

With all of the contradictions we have outlined throughout this book in mind, we want to end by considering—alongside so many other scholars, activists, artists, and organizers—the possibilities *and* limitations of the frame of decoloniality and anti-colonialism when it comes to self-care. This particular self-care moment seems ripe for (and very much in need of) a framework such as this, but we do not take the application of such a frame lightly, nor do we want to metaphorize "decolonization" in the way that Tuck & Yang, in their famed 2012 essay, forewarn against. This is particularly so in light of the brutal and deleterious economic and financial realities of the global health and wellness industry.

60   Tuck & Yang (2012), p. 35.

The political economy of self-care is very real. It harms and imperils workers—many of whom are women of color in the Global South—in addition to harming land, water, and non-human animals. "Self-care" is thus not only rhetorically annoying or visually distasteful on Instagram; the associated industry has irreversible material consequences.

In his introduction to a cluster of essays centered around the theme "Decolonize X?" for *Post 45* published in the summer of 2021, Scott Challener critically intervenes in the recent calls to decolonize anything and everything from therapy, yoga, Thanksgiving, the syllabus, the classroom, your bookshelf, and even _decolonization_ itself. In this same dossier, Kelly Roberts argues that "decolonization" has become a stand-in for "political engagement" and that this structural redress is too often directed at objects, institutions, and canons, for instance—or "your mind." As many scholars associated with "the decolonial turn" have argued—and many before them, who might not be included in that particular canon—decolonization, just like coloniality, is a process, and it doesn't have a clear endpoint. And part of that, that messy disordering process, *is the very point.* However, there are also real actors involved, and considering their unequal and uneven subjectivities, positionalities, and locations must be part of our *politics of engagement*—which indicates, for Roberts, the "need to re-route our political aspirations through their historical material stakes."

Care—and the centering of carers and carees within political and material circumstances—has the power to do this re-routing, we think. As so many Black, Brown, Indigenous, poor, disabled, queer, and trans feminists have argued, care can be fully networked and coalesced, and its reciprocal, reproductive, and revolutionary potentials are endless. Capitalism and colonialism make "self-care" feel necessary simply to survive, but care itself also necessarily has the power to abolish those structures of inequality. Care thus may have a decoloniality, an anti-capitalism, a justice-seeking inherent within it—when it is truly politically engaged and (re-)routed.

So, when considering whether or not self-care can be decolonized, as we do in this book, it might be useful to stop thinking about "practicing self-care" entirely, and instead, think of care, more broadly, as a powerful act of resistance, and one that is fundamentally relational and collective. And decoloniality—when put in terms of actual people, doing actual things, with actual different amounts of privilege, who then work to reconfigure these differentials through mutual aid, collective direct action, and comradeship—may be an important part of the alchemy required to make it through the chaos of capitalism, colonialism, and their undoing.

As a final thought: another author in this *Decolonize!* series has called for white hipsters to be race traitors as a possible way to decolonize a certain kind of white affect and way of life.[61] We think something similar needs to happen with self-care (again: more *care*, less *self*).

Is it possible to be a *care traitor*?

Maybe this looks like less talk on Twitter, and more work IRL—for instance, protecting communities and their water, resources, and land, on the ground, in real time. Again, we are not here to naysay or call out woke influencers for not being pure or perfect enough. We are all enmeshed in the contradictions of neoliberal racial capitalism, and there is no obvious outside.

To put it more plainly: sometimes the seeming incommensurability between two different things or approaches or ideas doesn't just end in chaos and breakdown but rather helps bring about a break*through*—that is, through the tension, a new possibility is born.

61   Pierrot (2021).

Lilla Watson, Aboriginal elder, activist, and educator, has said: "If you have come to help me, you are wasting your time. If you have come because your liberation is bound up with mine, then let us work together." We want to end this book with this quote because we think it encompasses something much different than the neoliberal idea of caring for others because it makes you feel better about yourself. We believe there is a way to acknowledge our common need for liberation, while simultaneously acknowledging that we all have very different experiences of marginalization and oppression. Part of the work is embracing that collective need for care *and* putting down our defenses, remembering that different amounts and forms of care are needed for different people and different groups, at different times, and that's okay.

We, along with so many others, are trying to figure out how best to do the work of exiting capitalism, ending fascism, and abolishing colonialism, racism, cis-heterosexism, and white supremacy. And making real care more attainable for everyone is an important step in that direction, amidst all of the other work that has to be done. We believe that forms of care and social organization based on interdependence, reciprocity, and accountability (to one another, the land, and all creatures) are not only possible, but imperative—to a revolutionary politics, to a decolonial project, and for a better world. We hope our efforts here and in the future can be a small part of the work of creating these things.

Oh, and P.S.—along the way?—Universal Healthcare For All!

REFERENCES

Active Minds. (n.d.). Self-care and mental health. Retrieved July 20, 2022, from https://www.activeminds.org/about-mental-health/self-care/#:~:text=What%20is%20self%2Dcare%3F,fully%2C%20vibrantly%2C%20and%20effectively

Ahmed, S. (2010). *The promise of happiness*. Durham, NC: Duke University Press.

Alexander, M. J. (2005). *Pedagogies of crossing: Meditations on feminism, sexual politics, memory, and the sacred*. Durham, NC: Duke University Press.

American Academy of Allergy, Asthma, & Immunology. (n.d.). The myth of IGG food panel testing. https://www.aaaai.org/conditions-and-treatments/library/allergy-library/IgG-food-test

American Psychiatric Association. (2013). *Diagnostic and statistical manual of mental disorders* (5th ed.). Arlington, VA: Author.

American Psychiatric Association. (n.d.) APA Public opinion poll—Annual meeting 2018. https://www.psychiatry.org/newsroom/apa-public-opinion-poll-annual-meeting-2018

Appleton, N. S. (2019, February 4). 'Do not "decolonize" . . . If you are not decolonizing': Progressive language and planning beyond a hollow academic rebranding. *Critical Ethnic Studies Blog.* http://www. criticalethnicstudiesjournal.org/blog/2019/1/21/ do-not-decolonize-if-you-are-not-decolonizing- alternate-language-to-navigate-desires-for-progressive- academia-6y5sg

Arango, T. (2020, September 3). Just because I have a car doesn't mean I have enough money to buy food. *New York Times.* https://www.nytimes.com/2020/09/03/us/ food-pantries- hunger-us.html

Aultman, B. (2014). Cisgender. *TSQ*, 1(1-2), 61–62. https:// doi.org/10.1215/23289252-2399614

Anzaldúa, G. (1983). Forward to the second edition. *This bridge called my back: Writings by radical women of color.* In C. Moraga, G. Anzaldúa, & T.C. Bambara (Eds.). New York, NY: Kitchen Table / Women of Color Press.

Barkataki, S. (2015, February 7). How to decolonize your yoga practice. *Decolonizing Yoga.* https:// decolonizingyoga.com/decolonize-yoga-practice/

Barker, K. (2014). Mindfulness meditation: Do-it-yourself medicalization of every moment. *Social Science & Medicine*, 106, 168–176.

Basas, C. G. (2014). What's bad about wellness? What the disability rights perspective offers about the limitations of wellness. *Journal of Health Politics, Policy and Law*, 39(5), 1035–1066.

Bassett, M. T. (2016). Beyond berets: The Black Panthers as health activists. *American Journal of Public Health*, 106(10), 1741–1743.

Bassett, M. T. (2019). No justice, no health: The Black Panther Party's fight for health in Boston and beyond. *Journal of African American Studies*, 23, 352–363.

Basson, R. (2000). The female sexual response: A different model. *Journal of Sex & Marital Therapy*, 26, 51–65.

Bedell, D. (2018, June 12) Seeds of change: How women owners are driving business growth in the wellness sector. *This is Capitalism*. https://www.thisiscapitalism.com/seeds-of-change-how-women-owners-are-driving-business-growth-in-the-wellness-sector/

Beecher, C. & Beecher Stowe, H. (1869 [2002]). *The American woman's home*. Hartford, CT: Harriet Beecher Stowe Center.

Bell, W. (March 6, 2018). 9 self-care tips. *Teen Vogue*. https://www.teenvogue.com/gallery/free-self-care-gift-guide

Bergner, D. (2009, November 24). Women who want to want. *New York Times Magazine*. https://www.nytimes.com/2009/11/29/magazine/29sex-t.html

Bhutta, N., Chang, A. C., Dettling, L. J. & Hsu, J. W. (2020, September 28). Disparities in wealth by race and ethnicity in the 2019 Survey of Consumer Finances. *Board of Governors of the Federal Reserve System*. https://www.federalreserve.gov/econres/notes/feds-notes/disparities-in-wealth-by-race-and-ethnicity-in-the-2019-survey-of-consumer-finances-20200928.htm

Billock, J. (2018, May 22). Pain bias: The health inequality rarely discussed. *BBC*. https://www.bbc.com/future/

article/20180518-the-inequality-in-how-women-are-treated-for-pain

Biltekoff, C. (2007). The terror within: Obesity in post 9/11 US life. *American Studies*, 48(3), 2948.

Bivens, J. & Zipperer, B. (2020, August 26). Health insurance and the COVID-19 shock: What we know so far about health insurance losses and what it means for policy. *Economic Policy Institute*. https://www.epi.org/publication/health-insurance-and-the-covid-19-shock/

Bivens, J. & Mishel, L. (2015, September 2). Understanding the historic divergence between productivity and a typical worker's pay. *Economic Policy Institute*. https://www.epi.org/publication/understanding-the-historic-divergence-between-productivity-and-a-typical-workers-pay-why-it-matters-and-why-its-real/

Bloom, J. & Martin, W. E. (2013). *Black against empire: The history and politics of the Black Panther Party*. Berkeley, CA: University of California Press.

Boehm, M. (n.d.) Michaela Boehm personal website. https://www.michaelaboehm.com/

Boehm, M. (2018). *The wild woman's way: Unlock your full potential for pleasure, power, and fulfillment*. New York, NY: Atria/Enliven.

Bondi, L. & Laurie, N. (2005). Working the spaces of neoliberalism: Activism, professionalisation, and incorporation: Introduction. *Antipode*, 37(3), 393–401.

Borgo Egnazia. (n. d.). Borgo Egnazia website. https://www.borgoegnazia.com/?lang=en

Bossio, J., Basson, R., Driscoll, M., Correia, S., & Brotto, L. (2018). Mindfulness-based group therapy for men with situational erectile dysfunction: A mixed-methods feasibility analysis and pilot study. *Journal of Sexual Medicine*, 15, 1478–1490.

Bowles, N. (2019, November 7). How to feel nothing now, in order to feel more later: A day of dopamine fasting in San Francisco. *The New York Times*. https://www.nytimes.com/2019/11/07/style/dopamine-fasting.html

Boyle, S. (n.d.). Remembering the origins of the self-care movement. *Bust*. Retrieved July 20, 2022 from https://bust.com/feminism/194895-history-of-self-care-movement.html

Brenton, J. and Elliott, S. (2014). Undoing gender? The case of complementary and alternative medicine. *Sociology of Health & Illness*, 36, 91–107. doi:10.1111/1467-9566.12043

Brodesser-Akner, T. (2017, August 2). Losing it in the anti-dieting age. *The New York Times Magazine*. https://www.nytimes.com/2017/08/02/magazine/weight-watchers-oprah-losing-it-in-the-anti-dieting-age.html

Brodesser-Akner, T. (2018, July 25). How Goop's haters made Gwyneth Paltrow's company worth $250 million. *The New York Times*. https://www.nytimes.com/2018/07/25/magazine/big-business-gwyneth-paltrow-wellness.html

Brotto, L. A. (2011). Non-judgmental, present-moment, sex . . . as if your life depended on it. *Sexual and Relationship Therapy*, 26, 215–216.

Brotto, L. A. (2018). *Better sex through mindfulness: How women can cultivate desire.* Berkeley, CA: Greystone Books.

Brown, A. M. (2017). *Emergent strategy: Shaping change, changing worlds.* New York, NY: AK Press.

Brown, A. M. (2019). *Pleasure activism: The politics of feeling good.* New York, NY: AK Press.

Brown, P., Zavestoski, S., McCormick, S., Mayer, B., Morello-Frosch, R., & Gasior Altman, R. (2004). Embodied health movements: New approaches to social movements in health. *Sociology of Health & Illness, 26,* 50–80. doi:10.1111/j.1467-9566.2004.00378.x

Browne, R. (2018, October 30). Gwyneth Paltrow's lifestyle firm Goop reported to UK watchdogs over 'potentially dangerous' health advice. *CNBC.* https://www.cnbc.com/2018/10/29/gwyneth-paltrows-goop-reported-to-uk-watchdogs-overadvertising.html

Bulka, C. M., Davis, M. A., Karagas, M. R., Ahsan, H., & Argos, M. (2016). The unintended consequences of a gluten-free diet. *Epidemiology, 28*(3), c-25-c-25.

Bulletproof. (n.d.). https://www.bulletproof.com

Calvo, L., & Rueda Esquibel, C. R. (2016). Decolonize your diet: Plant-based Mexican-American recipes for health and healing [Kindle iOS version].

Cambridge Dictionary. (n.d.). Financial instrument. https://dictionary.cambridge.org/us/dictionary/english/financial-instrument

Cardenas, D. (2013). Let not thy food be confused with thy medicine: The Hippocratic misquotation.

e-SPEN Journal, 8(6), e260-e262. doi: 10.1016/j. clnme.2013.10.002

Chait, J. (2012, October 3). Paul Ryan fears the 30 percent. *New York Magazine*. https://nymag.com/intelligencer/2012/10/paul-ryan-fears-the-30-percent.html

Challener, S. (2021, July 30). Introduction: Not only a metaphor. From *Decolonize X?* in *Post45*. https://post45.org/2021/07/introduction-not-only-a-metaphor/

Chandanabhumma, P. P. & Narasimhan, S. (2020). Towards health equity and social justice: An applied framework of decolonization in health promotion. *Health Promotion International*, 35(4), 831–840, https://doi.org/10.1093/heapro/daz053

Chang, M. L. & Nowel, A. (2016). How to make stone soup: Is the 'paleo diet' a missed opportunity for anthropologists? *Evolutionary Anthropology*, 25, 228–231.

Chivers, M. L., Seto, M. C., Lalumière, M. L., Laan, E., & Grimbos, T. (2010). Agreement of self-reported and genital measures of sexual arousal in men and women: A meta-analysis. *Archives of Sexual Behavior*, 39, 5–56.

Cigna. (2018, May 1). Cigna study reveals loneliness at epidemic levels in America: Spotlight on the impact of loneliness in the US and potential root causes. https://www.multivu.com/players/English/8294451-cigna-us-loneliness-survey/

Clare, E. (2017). *Brilliant imperfections: Grappling with cure*. Durham, NC: Duke University Press.

Cobra, S. (n.d.). Sasha Cobra personal website. https://www.sashacobra.com/

Conrad, P. (1994). Wellness as virtue: Morality and the pursuit of health. *Culture, Medicine, & Psychology*, 18, 385–401. https://doi.org/10.1007/BF01379232.

Crawford, R. (1980). Healthism and the medicalization of everyday life. *International Journal of Health Services*, 10(3), 365–388. https://doi.org/10.2190/3H2H-3XJN-3KAY-G9NY

Crawford, R. (2006). Health as a meaningful social practice. *Health*, 10(4), 401–420. https://doi.org/10.1177/1363459306067310.

Csikszentmihalyi, M. (1990). *Flow: The psychology of optimal experience*. New York, NY: Harper Perennial.

Curiel-Allen, T. (2018, March 4). What decolonization is, and what it means to me. *Teen Vogue*. https://www.teenvogue.com/story/what-decolonization-is-and-what-it-means-to-me

Cusens, B., Duggan, G. B., Thorne, K. & Burch, V. (2010). Evaluation of the breathworks mindfulness-based pain management programme: Effects on well-being and multiple measures of mindfulness. *Clinical Psychology & Psychotherapy*, 17, 63–78.

Daedone, N. (2011, June 11). *Orgasm: The cure for hunger in the Western woman* [Video]. TEDxSF. https://www.youtube.com/watch?v=s9QVq0EM6g4

Debiec, J. (2018, May 10). 39% of Americans more anxious today than this time last year. *Michigan Medicine – University of Michigan*. https://labblog.uofmhealth.org/body-work/39-of-americans-more-anxious-today-than-time-last-year

Deluca, A. N. (2013, November 1). Who multitasks best? Women, of course. *National Geographic*. https://www.nationalgeographic.com/science/article/131101-multitasking-women-productivity-psychology

Derkatch, C. (2018). The self-generating language of wellness and natural health. *Rhetoric of Health & Medicine*, 1(1), 132–160. https://www.muse.jhu.edu/article/710565

Desai, N. (2022). *The principles of pleasure* [Documentary TV series]. US: Netflix.

Desai, S. (2014, March 4). Gulabi Gang: India's women warriors. *Al Jazeera*. https://www.aljazeera.com/features/2014/03/04/gulabi-gang-indias-women-warriors/

Deutsch, T. (2010). *Building a housewife's paradise: Gender, politics, and American grocery stores in the twentieth century*. Chapel Hill, NC: University of North Carolina Press.

Dhamoon, R. K. (2009). Democracy, accountability, and disruption. In S. Gaon (Ed.), *Democracy in crisis: Violence, alterity, community*, (pp. 241–261). Manchester, UK: Manchester University Press.

DiGiacomo, D. V., Tennyson, C. A., Green, P. H., & Demmer, R. T. (2013). Prevalence of gluten-free diet adherence among individuals without celiac disease in the USA: Results from the Continuous National Health and Nutrition Examination Survey, 2009-2010. *Scandinavian Journal of Gastroenterology*, 48, 921–925.

Don't Mess with Mama. (n.d.). https://dontmesswithmama.com/blog/

Druckerman, K. (2020). *(Un)Well* [Documentary TV series]. US: Left/Right Productions.

Du Bois, W. E. B. (1899). *The Philadelphia Negro: A social study*. Philadelphia, PA: University of Pennsylvania Press.

Esquibel, C. R. (2016). Decolonize your diet: Notes toward decolonization. *Food First*. https://foodfirst.org/publication/decolonize-your-diet-notes-towards-decolonization/

EZLN (Zapatista Army of National Liberation). (2005). *The Sixth Declaration of the Selva Lacandona*. https://enlacezapatista.ezln.org.mx/sdsl-en/

Fair Trade Certified. (n.d.). It's time for the world to start caring about coconuts. https://www.fairtradecertified.org/news/power-of-coconut

Federal Trade Commission (2017, April 19). FTC staff reminds influencers and brands to clearly disclose relationship. https://www.ftc.gov/news-events/press-releases/2017/04/ftc-staff-reminds-influencers-brands-clearly-disclose

Federici, S. (2004). *Caliban and the witch: Women, the body and primitive accumulation*. New York, NY: Autonomedia.

Federici, S. (2012). *Revolution at point zero: Housework, reproduction, and feminist struggle*. New York, NY: PM Press.

Forrest, C. (2018). Choosing between paleo, keto, Whole30, vegan, & clean eating diets. *Clean Eating Kitchen*. https://www.cleaneatingkitchen.com/paleo-keto-whole30-vegan-diets/

Fox, S. (2014). The social life of health information. *Pew Research Center.* https://www.pewresearch.org/fact-tank/2014/01/15/the-social-life-of-health-information/

Freudenberg, N. (2014). *Lethal but legal: Corporations, consumption, and protecting public health* [Kindle iOS version].

Fullilove, M.T. (2004). *Root shock: How tearing up city neighborhoods hurts America, and what we can do about it.* New York, NY: One World / Ballantine Books.

Gaesser, G. A. & Angadi, S. S. (2012). Gluten-free diet: Imprudent dietary advice for the general population? *Journal of the Academy of Nutrition and Dietetics,* 112(9), 1330–1333.

Gans, K. (2019). The 10 most popular diets of 2018, according to Google. *US News and World Report.* https://health.usnews.com/health-news/blogs/eat-run/articles/2019-01-15/the-10-most-popular-diets-of-2018-according-to-google (accessed October 31, 2020).

Getachew, Y., Zephyrin, L., Abrams, M. K., Shah, A., Lewis, C. & Doty, M. M. (2020, September 10). Beyond the case count: The wide-ranging disparities of COVID-19 in the United States. *Commonwealth Fund.* https://www.commonwealthfund.org/publications/2020/sep/beyond-case-count-disparities-covid-19-united-states

Global Entrepreneurship Monitor (GEM). 2018/2019 Global Report, https://www.gemconsortium.org/report/gem-2018-2019-global-report

Global Entrepreneurship Monitor (GEM). 2019/2020 Global Report, https://www.gemconsortium.org/file/open?fileId=50443

Global Entrepreneurship Monitor (GEM). 2019/2020 United States Report, https://www.gemconsortium.org/file/open?fileId=50518

Global Entrepreneurship Monitor (GEM). 2016/2017 Women's Entrepreneurship Report, https://www.babson.edu/media/babson/site-assets/content-assets/images/news/announcements/GEM-2016-2017-Womens-Report.pdf

Global Wellness Institute (GWI). Global Wellness Economy Monitor, October 2018, https://globalwellnessinstitute.org/wp-content/uploads/2018/10/Research2018_v5webfinal.pdf

Global Wellness Summit (GWS). 2018 Global Wellness Trends Report, https://www.globalwellnesssummit.com/2018-global-wellness-trends/

Goldman, E. (1931). *Living my life*. New York, NY: Knopf.

Goldemeier, D. (2013). Mindfulness: A sexual medicine physician's personal and professional journey. *Sexual and Relationship Therapy*, 28, 77–83.

Goldstein, M. S. (2002). The emerging socioeconomic and political support for alternative medicine in the United States. *The Annals of the American Academy of Political and Social Science*, 583(1), 44–63.

Graham, J. (2017). *Good sex: Getting off without checking out*. Berkeley, CA: North Atlantic Books.

Gregg, M. (2018). *Counterproductive: Time management in the knowledge economy.* Durham, NC: Duke University Press.

Gumbs, A. P., Martens, C., & Williams, M. (Eds). (2016). *Revolutionary mothering: Love on the front lines.* Oakland, CA: PM Press.

Gunter, J. (2019, July 26). 'No, Goop, we are most definitely not on the same side.' *Dr. Jen Gunter's Personal Blog/ Website.* https://drjengunter.com/2019/07/26/no-goop-we-are-most-definitely-not-on-the-same-side/

Gunter, J. (2019). *The vagina bible: The vulva and vagina— separating the myth from the medicine.* New York, NY: Citadel Press.

Guthman, J. (2011). *Weighing in: Obesity, food justice, and the limits of capitalism.* Berkeley, CA: University of California Press.

Haber, A. & Ballantyne, S. (2015). *The healing kitchen: 175+ quick & easy paleo recipes to help you thrive.* Las Vegas, NV: Victory Belt Publishing.

Hanna, K. B. (2020). 'Centerwomen' and the 'Fourth Shift': Hidden figures of transnational Filipino activism in Los Angeles, 1972-1992. In R. M. Rodriguez (Ed.), *Filipino American Transnational Activism: Diasporic Politics among the Second Generation* (pp. 146–170). Boston, MA: Brill Publishing.

Harris, A. (2017, April 5). A history of self-care: From its radical roots to its yuppie-driven middle age to its election-inspired resurgence. *Slate.* http://www.slate.

com/articles/arts/culturebox/2017/04/the_history_of_
self_care.html

Harris, C. (1993). Whiteness as property. *Harvard Law
Review,* 106(8), 1707–1791. doi:10.2307/1341787.

Hartman, S. (1997). *Scenes of subjection: Terror, slavery, and
self-making in nineteenth-century America.* New York, NY:
Oxford University Press.

Hartwig, D. & Harwig, M. (2012). *It starts with food: Discover
the Whole30 and change your life in unexpected ways.* Las
Vegas, NV: Victory Belt Publishing.

Hassan, A. (2019, November 12). Hate-crime violence hits
16-year high, FBI reports. *New York Times.* https://
www.nytimes.com/2019/11/12/us/hate-crimes-fbi-
report.html

Health Resources & Services Administration. (2019, January
17). The 'loneliness epidemic.' https://www.hrsa.gov/
enews/past-issues/2019/january-17/loneliness-epidemic

Hess, A. (2020, March 17). The Wing is a women's utopia.
Unless you work there. *The New York Times.* https://
www.nytimes.com/2020/03/17/magazine/the-wing.
html

Hesse, M. (2019, April 11). The key to glorifying a
questionable diet? Be a tech bro and call it 'biohacking.'
The Washington Post. https://www.washingtonpost.
com/lifestyle/style/the-key-to-glorifying-a-
questionable-diet-be-a-tech-bro-and-call-it-
biohacking/2019/04/11/12368e2c-5ba2-11e9-842d-
7d3ed7eb3957_story.html?utm_source=reddit.com

Hill, L. (2019, October 17). Global wellness industry now worth $4.5 trillion, thanks to $828 billion physical activity market. *WellToDo: Global Wellness News*. https://www.welltodoglobal.com/global-wellness-industry-now-worth-4-5-trillion-thanks-to-828-billion-physical-activity-market/

Hobart, H. J. K. & Kneese, T. (2020). Radical care: Survival strategies for uncertain times. *Social Text*, 142, 38(1), 1–16.

Huet, E. (2018, June 18). The dark side of the Orgasmic Meditation company. *Bloomberg Businessweek*. https://www.bloomberg.com/news/features/2018-06-18/the-dark-side-of-onetaste-the-orgasmic-meditation-company

Hyman, M. (2018). *Food: What the heck should I eat*. New York, NY: Little, Brown and Company.

Jacobs, A. (2017, June 14). Meet the Goopies. *The New York Times*. https://www.nytimes.com/2017/06/14/fashion/gwyneth-paltrow-in-goop-health-wellness.html?module=Uisil

Jaime, A. (2019, August 8). True self-care is not about you. *VICE*. https://www.vice.com/en_us/article/ywazwb/true-self-care-is-not-about-you

Kaba, M. (2019, January 3). Black women punished for self-defense must be freed from their cages. *The Guardian*. https://www.theguardian.com/commentisfree/2019/jan/03/cyntoia-brown-marissa-alexander-black-women-self-defense-prison

Kaplan, L. (1995). *The story of Jane: The legendary underground feminist abortion service*. Chicago, IL: University of Chicago Press.

Karavolias, N. (2019, May 9). Organic food is booming, but it's grinding field laborers into the dirt. *Massive Science*. https://massivesci.com/articles/organic-farming-food-usda-pesticide-agricultural-labor/

Kincaid, J. (2000). *A small place*. New York, NY: Farrar, Straus, & Giroux.

Kisner, J. (2017, March 14). The politics of conspicuous displays of self-care. *The New Yorker*. https://www.newyorker.com/culture/culture-desk/the-politics-of-selfcare

Knight, C. (2015). We can't go back a hundred million years. *Food, Culture & Society*, 18(3), 441–461, doi:10.1080/15528014.2015.1043107

Knoll, J. (2019, June 8). Smash the wellness industry. *The New York Times*. https://www.nytimes.com/2019/06/08/opinion/sunday/women-dieting-wellness.html

Kochhar, R. (2020, June 11). Unemployment rose higher in three months of COVID-19 than it did in two years of the Great Recession. *Pew Research Center*. https://www.pewresearch.org/fact-tank/2020/06/11/unemployment-rose-higher-in-three-months-of-covid-19-than-it-did-in-two-years-of-the-great-recession/

Kochhar, R. & Cilluffo, A. (2018, July 12). Income inequality in the US is rising most rapidly among Asians. *Pew Research Center*. https://www.

pewsocialtrends.org/2018/07/12/income-inequality-in-the-u-s-is-rising-most-rapidly-among-asians/

Kochhar, R. & Cilluffo, A. (2017, November 1). How wealth inequality has changed in the US since the Great Recession, by race, ethnicity and income. *Pew Research Center.* https://www.pewresearch.org/fact-tank/2017/11/01/how-wealth-inequality-has-changed-in-the-u-s-since-the-great-recession-by-race-ethnicity-and-income/

Koscis, A., & Newbury-Helps, J. (2016). Mindfulness in sex therapy and intimate relationships (MSIR): Clinical protocol and theory development. *Mindfulness*, 7, 690–699.

Kotecki, P. (2019, January 2). The most popular diets millennials want to try in 2019. *Business Insider.* https://www.businessinsider.com/most-popular-diets-millennials-want-to-try-2019-2018-12

Kowitt, B. (2015, May 21). Special report: The war on big food. *Fortune.* https://fortune.com/2015/05/21/the-war-on-big-food/

Kresser, C. (2017). *Unconventional medicine: Join the revolution to reinvent health care, reverse chronic disease, and create a practice you love.* Lioncrest Publishing.

Kresser Institute. (n.d.). https://kresserinstitute.com/

Larocca, A. (2017). The wellness epidemic: Why are so many privileged people feeling so sick? Luckily, there's no shortage of cures. *The Cut.* https://www.thecut.com/2017/06/how-wellness-became-an-epidemic.html

Laudan, R. (2001). A plea for culinary modernism: Why we should love new, fast, processed food. *Gastronomica*, 1(1), 36–44.

Levenstein, H. (2012). *Fear of food: A history of why we worry about what we eat.* Chicago, IL: University of Chicago Press.

Lewis, C. H. (2005). Waking Sleeping Beauty: The premarital pelvic exam and heterosexuality during the Cold War. *Journal of Women's History*, 17, 86–110.

Lewis, S. (2019). *Full surrogacy now: Feminism against family.* New York, NY: Verso Books.

Linehan, M. M. (1993). *Cognitive-behavioral treatment of borderline personality disorder.* New York, NY: Guilford Press.

Lis, D. M., Stellingwerff, T., Shing, C. M., Ahuja, K. D. K., & Fell, J. W. (2014). Exploring the popularity, experiences, and beliefs surrounding gluten-free diets in nonceliac athletes. *International Journal of Sport Nutrition and Exercise Metabolism*, 25, 37–45.

Lorde, A. (1984). *Sister outsider: Essays and speeches by Audre Lorde.* Berkeley, CA: Crossing Press.

Lorde, A. (1988). *A burst of light and other essays.* Ithaca, NY: Firebrand Books.

Lopez, S. (2020, July 4). Column: Out of work, desperate and hungry, they waited in long lines for food. *Los Angeles Times.* https://www. latimes.com/california/story/2020-07-04/ food-banks-desperation-coronavirus-unemployment

Lugones, M. (2007). Heterosexualism and the colonial/
    modern gender system. *Hypatia*, 22(1), 186–209.

Lugones, M. (2010). Toward a decolonial feminism. *Hypatia*,
    25(4), 742–759.

Maldonado-Torres, N. (2016, October 23). Outline of
    ten theses on coloniality and decoloniality. *Franz
    Fanon Foundation*. https://fondation-frantzfanon.com/
    wp-content/uploads/2018/10/maldonado-torres_
    outline_of_ten_theses-10.23.16.pdf

Markowitz, S. (2001). Pelvic politics: Sexual dimorphism
    and racial difference. *Signs*, 26, 389–414.

Marquez, P. V. (2017, January 12). Healthy women
    are the cornerstone of healthy societies. *World
    Bank Blogs*. https://blogs.worldbank.org/health/
    healthy-women-are-cornerstone-healthy-societies

Marya, R. (n.d.). Decolonizing health care:
    Addressing social stressors in medicine. *Bioneers*.
    https://bioneers.org/decolonizing-health
    care-addressing-social-stressors-in-medicine-ztvz1812/

Martin, D. (2003, April 18). Dr. Robert C. Atkins, author
    of controversial but best-selling diet books, is dead
    at 72. *The New York Times*. https://www.nytimes.
    com/2003/04/18/nyregion/dr-robert-c-atkins-author-
    controversial-but-best-selling-diet-books-dead-72.html

Massey, D. S., & Denton, N. A. (1993). *American apartheid:
    Segregation and the making of the underclass*. Cambridge,
    MA: Harvard University Press.

Masters, W. H., & Johnson, V. E. (1966). *Human sexual
    response*. New York, NY: Bantam Books.

Mayorga, E., Leidecker, L. & Orr de Gutierrez, D. (2019). Burn it down: The incommensurability of the university and decolonization. *Journal of Critical Thought and Praxis*, 8(1), 87–106.

McWhorter, L. (2004). Sex, race, and biopower: A Foucauldian genealogy. *Hypatia*, 19, 38–62.

McWhorter, L. (2009). *Racism and sexual oppression in Anglo-America: A genealogy*. Bloomington, IN: Indiana University Press.

McGee, M. (2020). Capitalism's care problem: Some traces, fixes, and patches. *Social Text* 142, 38(1), 39–66.

Melamed, J. (2006). The spirit of neoliberalism from racial liberalism to neoliberal multiculturalism. *Social Text*, 24(4_89), 1–24.

Meltzer, M. (2016, December 10). Soak, steam, spritz: It's all self-care. *The New York Times*. https://www.nytimes.com/2016/12/10/fashion/post-election-anxiety-self-care.html

Mies, M. & Bennholdt-Thomsen, V. (1999). *The subsistence perspective: Beyond the globalised economy*. London, UK: Zed Books.

Mickey, E. L. (2019). "'Eat, pray, love' bullshit": Women's empowerment through wellness at an elite professional conference. *Journal of Contemporary Ethnography*, 48(1), 103–127. https://doi.org/10.1177/0891241617752409

Miller, J. (2020, May 29). An ode to mac and cheese, the poster child for processed food. *Colorado State University homepage*. https://source.colostate.edu/an-ode-to-mac-and-cheese-the-poster-child-for-processed-food/

Mintz, L. B. (2009). *A tired woman's guide to passionate sex: Reclaim your desire and reignite your relationship.* Avon, MA: Adams Media.

Moore, L. R. (2014). 'But we're not hypochondriacs:' The changing shape of gluten-free dieting and the contested illness experience. *Social Science and Medicine*, 105, 76–83.

Morini, C. (2007). The feminization of labour in cognitive capitalism. *Feminist Review*, 87, 40–59.

Moss, G. (2016). *Glop: Nontoxic, expensive ideas that will make you look ridiculous and feel pretentious.* New York, NY: Dey Street Books.

Movement for Black Lives. (n.d.). https://m4bl.org/

Mull, A. (2018, October 30). The harder, better, faster, stronger language of dieting. *The Atlantic.* https://www.theatlantic.com/health/archive/2018/10/tech-industry-diet-products-have-whole-new-language/574390/?gclid=Cj0KCQjwlvT8BRDeARIsAACRFiUN4YzBKz-NGZGmI6S77OkbgLzpRkJIzXXx6QYovq73-evf1FX5NhwaAqfHEALw_wcB

Murphy, M. (2012). *Seizing the means of reproduction: Entanglements of feminism, health, and technoscience.* Durham, NC: Duke University Press.

Murphy, M. (2017). *The economization of life.* Durham, NC: Duke University Press.

Mzezewa, T. (2021, July 27). The travel industry's reckoning with race and inclusion. *The New York Times.* https://www.nytimes.com/2021/07/27/travel/black-travelers-diversity-inclusion.html

National Archives. (n.d.). The Homestead Act of 1862. https://www.archives.gov/education/lessons/homestead-act

National Public Radio. (2020, October 8). Pandemic 'profiteers:' Why billionaires are getting richer during an economic crisis. https://www.npr.org/2020/10/05/920314309/pandemic-profiteers-why-billionaires-are-getting-richer-during-an-economic-crisis

Nelson, A. (2013). *Body and soul: The Black Panther Party and the fight against medical discrimination.* Minneapolis, MN: University of Minnesota Press.

Newberry, C., McKnight, L, Sarav, M., & Pickett-Blakely, O. (2017). Going gluten-free: The history and nutritional implications of today's most popular diet. *Current Gastroenterology Reports*, 19, 54. https://doi.org/10.1007/s11894-017-0597-2

Ngũgĩ wa Thiong'o. (1986). *Decolonising the Mind: The Politics of Language in African Literature.* Nairobi, Kenya/Suffolk, UK: East African Educational Publishers/James Currey.

Ochoa Ayala, M. (2020, February 24). Avocado: the 'green gold' causing environmental havoc. *World Economic Forum*. https://www.weforum.org/agenda/2020/02/avocado-environment-cost-food-mexico/

O'Neill, R. (2020). Pursuing 'wellness:' Considerations for Media Studies. *Television & New Media*, 21, 628–634.

Otterman, S. (2019, April 12). A white restauranteur advertised 'clean' Chinese food. Chinese-Americans

had something to say about it. *The New York Times.*
https://www.nytimes.com/2019/04/12/nyregion/
lucky-lees-nyc-chinese-food.html

Owens, D. C. (2017). *Medical bondage: Race, gender, and the origins of American gynecology.* Athens, GA: University of Georgia Press.

Parr, H. (2002). New body-geographies: The embodied spaces of health and medical information on the internet. *Environment and Planning D: Society and Space,* 20(1), 73–95. doi:10.1068/d41j

Parsley Health. (n.d.). www.parsleyhealth.com

Penny, L. (2016, July 8). Life-hacks of the poor and aimless: On negotiating the false idols of neoliberal self-care. *The Baffler.* https://thebaffler.com/latest/laurie-penny-self-care

People's Collective Kitchen. (n.d.). http://peopleskitchencollective.com/

Perlmutter, D. (2014). *Grain brain: The surprising truth about wheat, carbs, and sugar—your brain's silent killers.* New York, NY: Yellow Kite.

Perrier, M. & Swan, E. (2019, December 9). Foodwork: Racialized, gendered, and classed labours. *Futures of Work.* https://futuresofwork.co.uk/2019/12/09/foodwork-racialised-gendered-and-class-labours/

Petersen, A. R., Davis, M., Fraser, S. & Lindsay, J. (2010). Healthy living and citizenship: An overview. *Critical Public Health,* 20(4), 391–400.

Petersen, A. R. & Lupton, D. (1996). *The new public health: Health and self in the age of risk.* London: SAGE.

Pew Research Center. (2018). The internet and health. https://www.pewresearch.org/internet/2013/02/12/the-internet-and-health/

Piepzna-Samarasinha, L. L. (2018). *Care work: Dreaming disability justice*. Vancouver, BC: Arsenal Pulp Press.

Povinelli, E. A. (2011). *Economies of abandonment: Social belonging and endurance in late liberalism*. Durham, NC: Duke University Press.

Purser, R. (2019, June 14). The mindfulness conspiracy. *The Guardian*. https://www.theguardian.com/lifeandstyle/2019/jun/14/the-mindfulness-conspiracy-capitalist-spirituality

Quijano, A. (2000). Coloniality of power, eurocentrism, and Latin America. *Nepantla: Views from the South*, 1(3), 533–580.

Quijano, A. & Wallerstein, I. (1992). Americanity as a concept, or the Americas in the modern world-system. *International Social Science Journal*, 134, 549–557.

Rainsborough, J. (2011). *Lifestyle media and the formation of the self*. New York, NY: Palgrave Macmillan.

Raphael, R. (2018, October 8). These 10 market trends turned wellness into a $4.2 trillion global Industry. *Fast Company*. https://www.fastcompany.com/90247896/these-10-market-trends-turned-wellness-into-a-4-2-trillion-global-industry

Reich, J. A. (2016). Of natural bodies and antibodies: Parents' vaccine refusal and the dichotomies of natural and artificial. *Social Science and Medicine*, 157, 103–110.

Reisner, S. L., White Hughto, J. M., Gamarel, K. E., Keuroghlian, A. S., Mizock, L., & Pachankis, J.

(2016). Discriminatory experiences associated with posttraumatic stress disorder symptoms among transgender adults. *Journal of Counseling Psychology*, 63(5), 509–519.

Richards, E. (1882). *The chemistry of cooking and cleaning.* Boston, MA: Whitcomb & Barrows.

Richards, E. (1904). *The art of right living.* Boston, MA: Whitcomb & Barrows.

Richardson, D. (2003). *The heart of Tantric sex: A unique guide to love and sexual fulfillment.* Hants, UK: O Books.

Richardson, D. (2011). *Slow sex: The path to fulfilling and sustainable sexuality.* Rochester, VT: Destiny Books.

Richardson, D. (2018, April 2). *The power of mindful sex* [Video]. TEDxLinz. https://www.youtube.com/watch?v=oqyW35EMLuM&list=PLs3Kdx4uDYWRwVkPLi7pA9rE2Q-D-Mhc5&index=41&t=0s

Roberts, D. (1997). *Killing the black body: Race, reproduction, and the meaning of liberty.* New York, NY: Vintage Books.

Roberts, K. (2021, August 10). "X, Decolonize." From *Decolonize X?* in *Post45*. https://post45.org/2021/08/x-decolonize/

Rosman, K. (2020, June 11). Audrey Gelman, The Wing's co-founder, resigns. *The New York* Times. https://www.nytimes.com/2020/06/11/style/the-wing-ceo-audrey-gelman-resigns.html

Rottenberg, C. (2013). The rise of neoliberal feminism. *Cultural Studies*, 28(3), 418–37.

Rottenberg, C. (2020). *The rise of neoliberal feminism.* Oxford, UK: Oxford University Press.

Rowland, K. (2020). *The pleasure gap: American women and the unfinished sexual revolution.* New York, NY: Seal Press.

Rythmia Life Advancement Center. (n.d.). https://www.rythmia.com/

Saad, L. (2019, September 13). What percentage of Americans own stock? Gallup. https://news.gallup.com/poll/266807/percentage-americans-owns-stock.aspx

Sainato, M. (2019, July 16). Whole Foods workers say conditions deteriorated after Amazon takeover. *The Guardian.* https://www.theguardian.com/business/2019/jul/16/whole-foods-amazon-prime-working-conditions

Saito, N. T. (2015, February 26). Race and decolonization: Whiteness as property in the American settler colonial project. *Harvard Journal on Racial & Ethnic Justice.* http://ssrn.com/abstract=2593121

Sandoval, C. (2000). *Methodology of the oppressed.* Minneapolis, MN: University of Minnesota Press.

Schlosser, K. (2020, September 16). Bulletproof raises $13M to fuel growth of 'high performance' food and beverage products. *GeekWire.* https://www.geekwire.com/2020/bulletproof-raises-13m-fuel-continued-growth-food-beverage-products/

Scholz, T. (2016). *Platform cooperativism: Challenging the corporate sharing economy.* New York, NY: Rosa Luxemburg.

Scott, E. (2020, August 3). 5 self-care practices for every area of your life. VeryWell Mind. https://www.verywellmind.com/self-care-strategies-overall-stress-reduction-3144729

Segal, Z. V., Williams, J. M. G., & Teasdale, J. D. (2002). *Mindfulness-based cognitive therapy for depression: A new approach to preventing relapse*. New York, NY: Guilford.

Seiler, C. (2020). The origins of white care. *Social Text*, 142, 38(1), 17–38.

Self-care. (n.d.) In *Wikipedia*. Retrieved July 21, 2022, from https://en.wikipedia.org/wiki/Self-care

Self Practice Blog. (2020, June 15). Angela Davis on radical self care. https://www.selfpractice.com.au/self-practice/angela-davis-on-radical-self-care

Selva, J. (2020, December 10). Top 50 best mindfulness books. *Positive Psychology*. https://positivepsychology.com/mindfulness-books/

Sitrin, M. (2006). *Horizontalism: Voices of popular power in Argentina*. New York, NY: AK Press.

Snorton, C. R. (2017). *Black on both sides: A racial history of trans identity*. Minneapolis, MN: University of Minnesota.

Somerville, S. (1994). Scientific racism and the emergence of the homosexual body. *Journal of the History of Sexuality*, 5, 243–266.

Somerville, S. (2000). *Queering the color line: Race and the invention of homosexuality in American culture*. Durham, NC: Duke University Press.

Sonfield, A., Frost, J. J., Dawson, R. & Lindberg, L. D. (2020, August 3). COVID-19 job losses threaten insurance coverage and access to reproductive health care for millions. *Health Affairs*. https://www.healthaffairs.org/do/10.1377/forefront.20200728.779022/full/

Spade, D. (2020). *Mutual aid: Building solidarity during this crisis (and the next).* New York, NY: Verso Books.

Spade, D. (2020). Solidarity not charity: Mutual aid for mobilization and survival. *Social Text*, 142, 38(1), 131–151.

Spechler, D. (2016, November 11). The rise of Donald Trump demands we embrace a harder kind of self-care. *Quartz*. https://qz.com/834607/the-rise-of-donald-trump-demands-a-new-kind-of-self-care/

Spillers, H. (1987). Mama's baby, Papa's maybe: An American grammar book. *Diacritics*, 17, 64–81.

Spurgas, A. K. (2020). *Diagnosing desire: Biopolitics and femininity into the twenty-first century.* Columbus, OH: The Ohio State University Press.

Spurgas, A. K. (2021). Solidarity in falling apart: Toward a crip, collectivist, and justice-seeking theory of feminine fracture. *Lateral*, 10.1. https://csalateral.org/section/cripistemologies-of-crisis/solidarity-falling-apart-toward-crip-collectivist-justice-theory-feminine-fracture-spurgas/

Sreenivasan, H., Weber, S, & Kargbo, C. (2019, June 1). The true story beyond the 'welfare queen' stereotype. *PBS News Hour.* https://www.pbs.org/newshour/show/the-true-story-behind-the-welfare-queen-stereotype

Srnicek, N. (2016). *Platform capitalism*. Cambridge, UK: Polity.

Stackpole, T. (2019, July 11). You call it starvation. I call it biohacking. *The New York Times*. https://www.nytimes.com/2019/07/11/opinion/sunday/men-extreme-diets.html?referringSource=articleShare

Stamp, N. (2019, May 23). The revolutionary origins of self-care. *Local Love*. https://locallove.ca/issues/the-revolutionary-origins-of-self-care/#.X0quSGdKjEZ

Stiglitz, J. E. (2012). *The price of inequality: How today's divided society endangers our future*. New York, NY: W.W. Norton & Company.

Stone, C., Trisi, D., Sherman, A. & Beltrán, J. (2020, January 13). A guide to statistics on historical trends in income inequality. *Center for Budget and Policy Priorities*. https://www.cbpp.org/research/poverty-and-inequality/a-guide-to-statistics-on-historical-trends-in-income-inequality

Strangers in a Tangled Wilderness. (2015). *A small key can open a large door: The Rojava revolution*. Strangers in a Tangled Wilderness Press.

Strom, S. (2014, April 25). As parents make their own baby food, industry tries to adapt. *The New York Times*. https://www.nytimes.com/2014/04/26/business/as-parents-make-their-own-industry-tries-to-adapt.html

Stuckler, D. & Nestle, M. (2012). Big food, big systems, and global health. *PLoS Medicine*, 9(6), e1001242.

Sykes, P. (2017, October 23). How BFF marketing became the M.O. for women's direct-to-consumer brands. *Business of Fashion*. https://www.businessoffashion.com/articles/intelligence/how-bff-marketing-became-the-m-o-for-womens-direct-to-consumer-brands

Tam, M. (2013). *Nom nom paleo: Food for humans*. Kansas City, MO: Andrews McMeel Publishing.

Taparia, H. & Koch, P. (2015, November 8). A seismic shift in how people eat. *The New York Times*. https://www.nytimes.com/2015/11/08/opinion/a-seismic-shift-in-how-people-eat.html

Tavakkoli, A., Lewis, S. K., Tennyson, C. A., Lebwohl, B., & Green, P. H. R. (2014). Characteristics of patients who avoid wheat and/or gluten in the absence of celiac disease. *Digestive Diseases and Sciences, 59*, 1255–1261.

Tech Crunch. (n.d.). The future of shopping is all about contextual commerce. https://techcrunch.com/sponsor/unlisted/the-future-of-shopping-is-all-about-contextual-commerce/?guccounter=1

The Care Collective. (2020). *Care manifesto: The politics of interdependence*. New York, NY: Verso Books.

The Coconut Mama. (n.d.). https://thecoconutmama.com/

The Feminine. (n.d.). https://www.thefeminine.com/

The Mommypotamus. (n.d.). https://mommypotamus.com/

The Paleo Mama. (n.d.). https://thepaleomama.com/

The Paleo Mom. (n.d.). https://www.thepaleomom.com/

The Paleo Running Momma. (n.d.). https://www.paleorunningmomma.com/

The Prairie Homestead. (n.d.). https://www.theprairiehomestead.com/

The Primal Blueprint. (n.d.). https://www.primalblueprint.com

The Wellness Mama. (n.d.). https://wellnessmama.com/

Thomashauer, R. (n.d.). Mama Gena personal website. http://mamagenas.com/

Tlostanova, M. V. & Mignolo, W. D. (2012). *Learning to unlearn: Decolonial reflections from Eurasia and the Americas.* Columbus, OH: The Ohio State University Press.

Tolentino, J. (2019). *Trick mirror: Reflections on self-delusion.* New York, NY: Random House.

Trombetta, S. (2018, January 2). Understanding the radical history of self-care is essential to practicing it successfully. *Hello Giggles.* https://hellogiggles.com/lifestyle/health-fitness/mental-health-advocates/

Tsipursky, G. (2018, July 5). (Dis)trust in science: Can we cure the scourge of misinformation? *Scientific American.* https://blogs.scientificamerican.com/observations/dis-trust-in-science/

Tuck, E. & Yang, K. W. (2012). Decolonization is not a metaphor. *Decolonization: Indigeneity, Education & Society*, 1(1), 1–40.

Tulshyan, R. (2021, July 29). No loans, no credit, no funding: Why more women aren't millionaires. *The New York Times.* https://www.nytimes.com/2021/07/29/us/we-should-all-be-millionaires-rachel-rodgers.html?searchResultPosition=6

United States Census Bureau (2016, March). Educational attainment in the United States: 2015. https://

www.census.gov/content/dam/Census/library/
publications/2016/demo/p20-578.pdf

United States Census Bureau (2020, September 15).
Race and poverty in the United States: 2019.
https://www.census.gov/library/publications/2020/
demo/p60-270.html

University of Michigan School of Public Health. (2020,
February 12). Healing in public health: Oppression,
trauma, and resilience: An interview with Kelly
Gonzales & Jilliene Joseph. https://sph.umich.edu/
pursuit/2020posts/healing-in-public-health.html

Wafai, Y., Larson, Z. & Pucci, C. (2019, July 2). 12 tips for
more equitable travel. *Yes!* https://www.yesmagazine.
org/issue/travel/2019/07/02/tips-vacation-social-justice

Walia, H. (2013). *Undoing border imperialism.* New York, NY:
AK Press.

Walia, H. (2021). *Border & rule: Global migration, capitalism,
and the rise of racist nationalism.* Chicago, IL: Haymarket
Books.

Walsh, C. E. & Mignolo, W. D. (Eds.). (2018). *On
decoloniality: Concepts, analytics, praxis.* Durham, NC:
Duke University Press.

Ward, J. (2020). *The tragedy of heterosexuality.* New York, NY:
New York University Press.

Washington, H. A. (2006). *Medical apartheid: The dark history
of medical experimentation on Black Americans from colonial
times to the present.* New York, NY: Broadway Books.

Weir, A. (2017). Decolonizing feminist freedom: Indigenous
relationalities. *Decolonizing feminism: Transnational*

feminism and globalization. In M.A. McLaren (Ed.) London, UK: Rowman & Littlefield.

Whole30 Community Cares Summit. (2020). https://hopin. to/events/whole30-ccs-2020#schedule

Whyte, K. P. (2016). Indigenous food sovereignty, renewal and US settler colonialism. *The Routledge Handbook of Food Ethics.* https://ssrn.com/abstract=2770056

Wilkes, K. (2021). Eating, looking, and living clean: Techniques of contemporary femininity in contemporary food culture. *Gender, Work, & Organization.* http://www.open-access.bcu.ac.uk/10721/

Wike, R., Silver, L. & Castillo, A. (2019, April 28). Many across the globe are dissatisfied with how democracy is working. *Pew Research Center.* https://www. pewresearch.org/global/2019/04/29/why-are-people-dissatisfied-with-how-democracy-is-working/

Wilson, J. (2017). 'Mindfulness makes you a way better lover:' Mindful sex and the adaptation of Buddhism to new cultural desires. In D. L. McMahan & E. Braun (Eds.). *Meditation, Buddhism, and Science* (pp. 152-172). Oxford, UK: Oxford University Press.

Zupello, S. (2019, February 15). The latest Instagram influencer frontier? Medical promotions. *Vox.* https:// www.vox.com/the-goods/2019/2/15/18211007/ medical-sponcon-instagram-influencer-pharmaceutical

ALYSON K. SPURGAS is Associate Professor of Sociology and affiliated faculty in the Women's, Gender, & Sexuality Studies Program at Trinity College in Hartford, Connecticut. Spurgas researches, writes, and teaches about the sociology of trauma, the politics of desire, and technologies of care from an interdisciplinary and intersectional feminist perspective. They are also the author of *Diagnosing Desire: Biopolitics and Femininity into the Twenty-First Century* (The Ohio State University Press, 2020), which won the 2021 Cultural Studies Association First Book Prize. Alyson lives in Brooklyn, New York, with their amazing partner and cat. Check out www.alysonkspurgas.com for info about Alyson's writing, teaching, speaking events, and more.

ZOË C. MELEO-ERWIN is a qualitative sociologist and former assistant professor of public health. In 2022, she left academia to pursue a career as a user experience researcher in the tech industry. As a scholar, her work focused on the meanings of health and illness, health decision-making, experiences of embodiment, and the ways in which digital technologies facilitate the creation of both identity and community around health and illness. A list of her publications can be found on her website, www.zoemeleoerwin.com.